# Thoreau's Downsizing Planner for Seniors

**Philip Baker**

Thoreau's Downsizing Planner for Seniors
Author: Philip Baker
Published by: Philip Baker

ISBN-13: 978-1547295890

ISBN-10: 1547295899

Thoreau's Downsizing Planner for Seniors

## This Downsizing Planner Belongs to:

## Table of Contents

# Section I. Using Thoreau's Downsizing Planner for Seniors

*"Our life is frittered away by detail... simplify, simplify."*
- Henry David Thoreau

## 1. How to Use This Planner

Moving is considered a high-stress life event. This relocation for seniors can be mixed with uncertainty, loneliness, possible illness, and a loss of independence. Due to the many additional decisions to be made for many seniors, downsizing can be more complex than just moving. Whether you or loved ones are moving across town or across the country, to a smaller home, or into a senior or care facility you will likely be:

- Tackling major living decisions.
- Visiting senior communities or care facilities and comparing options or shopping for a new home.
- Dealing with belongings; sorting through decades of family history, organizing, selling, giving way and discarding, and packing and unpacking.
- Organizing and cleaning.
- Selling, donating, and discarding items.
- Shutting off and turning on utilities.

- Stopping services and starting services.
- Changing addresses and notifying everyone
- Gathering, organizing and keeping important documents and records.

And with a myriad of other tasks all on a schedule, this is a formidable challenge for anyone and even paralyzing for many people.

*Thoreau's Downsizing Planner for Seniors* is designed to help seniors, empty nesters, children or relatives of seniors, and caregivers make this move easier through guiding information, organization and planning. If you are a caregiver or adult child helping your parent downsize, use this planner to help you be supportive, assist with choices, and have an efficient plan.

## Where You will Move

Whether you will be moving into a smaller home, apartment, care center, senior community, or a nursing home will dictate what belongings you will keep and those that you will not. Thoreau's Downsizing Planner for Seniors will explain these options.

## When to Start

A year is not too early to begin planning to trim your life by downsizing if you have the luxury of that much time. Depending on your situation you might have less time. In either case, this planner will help you make your

downsizing experience more organized and have a better outcome.

## Where to Start

Keep this planner with you from now and throughout your move and then as a collection of records if ever needed. Complete the to-do lists, calendars/timelines, 'notes to self', and anything you might forget.

There are lists, worksheets, and checklists designed for each step in this transition. ***Since every situation is different, select the chapters, areas and forms that apply to you.***

**Note:** Keep this planner with you, and whenever you think of something related to the move, write it down on the relevant form, worksheet, or in the 'Notes' section at the back of this planner.

# 2. Is Downsizing the Best Economic Move for You?

If you are downsizing to a smaller home this chapter will help you determine the economic outcome for your situation.

The average home in the U.S. has nearly tripled in size since the birth of the baby boom era. In 1950 the average home size as about 1,000 square feet. Now, even though the average family size is smaller, today's average home size is 2,600 square feet.

Often after moving up to a bigger house and filling room after room with more possessions, downsizing is a contrary idea and for many people a reverse in direction. For some people downsizing might seem like 'stepping down.' However, moving to a smaller home can be a 'step up' in your bank account. Reducing your belongings or in some cases clutter can also give you a better quality of life.

Living with smaller mortgage payments or none, lower utility bills and often paying less property taxes, is a welcome financial status for seniors in or facing retirement. However, you need to evaluate your situation and goals to discover if downsizing is really the right move for you.

While downsizing generally means more money in the bank and less expenses for most people, there are a few costly pitfalls you need to be aware of.

**Your Future**

Plan what will you need from a home in the next five to ten years. You want to avoid moving into a smaller space that cramps your style and drives you to buy a larger home again.

- Are you social?
- Do you throw parties?
- Will you be having family or other overnight guests at your home?
- Will you be needing in home care of any kind?
- Do you have pets?
- If you have pets what indoor and or outdoor space is required?
- In what area of your home do you spend the most time?
- How important is kitchen size to you?
- How many bathrooms will you need?
- Will you be working from home or starting a home-based business that will require space and if so, how much?

**Timing**

If you have the luxury of choosing then when you downsize could impact how you are affected financially.

Here are some questions to ask answer about downsizing and the timing:

- Is your home in a strong selling market currently?
- Are property values rapidly rising, stagnant, or falling?

- If you will be shopping for a new home what is the housing market like in that area?
- Will you be reinvesting any equity from your home into another property?
- Do you have family members that will soon be moving out of your home? For example, do you have children going off to college or to be married soon?
- Do you have any adult children that might circle back to the nest in the next few years?

## What are the Hidden Costs of Downsizing?

In addition to neglecting or miscalculating your future lifestyle there are some other expense considerations of downsizing.

Will your current home require repairs or other work before listing?

Property taxes can vary greatly between states and countries. Downsizing might cost you considerably more in property taxes depending on locations.

Will there be HOA fees at your new property?

If you are leaving a home that has no HOA fees to a community that does, this can be an added annual expense of thousands of dollars in some cases.

Although you might be selling possessions as part of your downsizing plan, will you need to be spending money to replace items or acquire new furniture, appliances, etc. for your new place?

Will your new home need changes, work or updating?

Remember to estimate the cost of your move and include that in the budget. In some instances, this could easily be several thousand dollars.

Will your new home have the same amenities as now or will you be paying for them after you move?

What might you be paying for that you are not now?

- Laundry service instead of facilities at home
- Gym membership instead of a home gym
- Car washing services versus washing your car at home now.

Will you need to travel differently or farther than you do now for services, recreation, groceries, doctors or other health specialists, and social events? If you walk to anything now that you will need to drive to that will be an added expense. Many seniors retire in the country or smaller towns or communities where they must travel longer distances for their needs.

Will you be giving up a car for other types of transportation and how will those costs compare?

Will you need to pay for any storage of belongings?

## What are the Financial Benefits of Downsizing?

While moving to a smaller home can lower or eliminate your mortgage payment, lower utility costs, require less home maintenance, and perhaps lower utility costs, there is also the use of saved money. Money you save by

downsizing can be invested or used to pay off debt. This often-overlooked benefit of use of savings can add up substantially.

1. Pay Off Debt

If you owe $18,000 with a 6% interest rate and a minimum payment of $200 a month, you will be paying on that loan for 10 more years. But pay an additional $500 each month and you could pay that off in less than three years!

2. Increase Your Retirement Fund

Invest $500 a month into a retirement account earning compound interest at 5% over ten years and you will earn about $25,000 with a balance of over $75,000 with no withdraws.

3. Pay Down Your Mortgage

If you do not pay in full or cash for your new home, get a 15-year mortgage with a fixed rate. If you are saving $500 a month from downsizing and apply that each month to your mortgage at a 4% interest rate you could pay a $200,000 mortgage in full in less than 11 years and save about $25,000 in interest.

## Estimating the Downsizing Financial Effects of Your Monthly Expenses

The following worksheets will help you determine how downsizing will affect your monthly budget.

While you might not know where you are going to move, you can complete the 'Worksheet B Expected (After Downsizing) Monthly Expenses' based on the budget you are aiming for. You can come back and do this portion again when you have accurate figures.

Note: You can get a printable copy of this form or any of the forms in this book at:

http://www.formgal.com/thoreauplanners.htm

## Current Monthly Expenses Worksheet A

| Current Monthly Home Ownership Expenses | |
| --- | --- |
| **Description** | **Monthly Amount** |
| All Utilities Average Monthly Cost | $ |
| Housing Cost (Mortgage, Rent, etc.) | $ |
| Private Mortgage Insurance (PMI) | $ |
| Home Maintenance Expenses | $ |
| Monthly Insurance Expense (Property, Renter's) | $ |
| Property Taxes (Monthly) | $ |
| Average Monthly Home Repairs | $ |
| Pest Control | $ |
| Lawn and Outdoor Maintenance | $ |
| HOA Fees | $ |
| Lawn Sprinkler System | $ |
| Swimming Pool | $ |
| | $ |
| | $ |
| | $ |
| **Total Home Ownership Expenses** (All Above) | **$** |

**Current Vehicle Ownership Expenses** (Only if you will be selling your vehicle or will be downsizing to one vehicle or a smaller vehicle)

| Description | Monthly Amount |
| --- | --- |
| Average Monthly Maintenance | $ |
| Monthly Fuel | $ |
| Monthly Loan or Lease Payment | $ |
| Monthly Auto Insurance | $ |
| Auto Taxes, License, Registration (Monthly Cost) | $ |
| Carwash and or Detail | $ |
| Parking Costs | $ |
| | $ |
| | $ |
| | $ |
| | $ |
| | $ |
| | $ |
| | $ |
| | |
| | |
| **Total Monthly Vehicle Expenses** | **$** |

| Current Services and Amenity Monthly Expenses | |
|---|---|
| **Description** | **Monthly Amount** |
| Gym Membership | $ |
| Golf or Country Club Membership | $ |
| Laundry Services | $ |
| Cleaning / Maid Service | $ |
| | $ |
| | $ |
| | $ |
| | $ |
| | $ |
| | $ |
| | $ |
| | $ |
| | $ |
| | $ |
| | $ |
| | $ |
| | $ |
| **Total Amenity Monthly Expenses:** | **$** |

## Expected (After Downsizing) Monthly Expenses Worksheet B

| Expected Monthly Home Ownership Expenses Worksheet B | |
|---|---|
| **Description** | **Monthly Amount** |
| All Utilities Average Monthly Cost | $ |
| Housing Cost (Mortgage, Rent, etc.) | $ |
| Private Mortgage Insurance (PMI) | $ |
| Home Maintenance Expenses | $ |
| Monthly Insurance Expense (Property, Renter's) | $ |
| Property Taxes (Monthly) | $ |
| Average Monthly Home Repairs | $ |
| Pest Control | $ |
| Lawn and Outdoor Maintenance | $ |
| HOA Fees | $ |
| Lawn Sprinkler System | $ |
| Swimming Pool | $ |
| | $ |
| | $ |
| **Total Expected Ownership Expenses** (All Above) | **$** |

**Expected Vehicle Ownership Expenses (Worksheet B)**
(Only if you will be selling your vehicle or will be downsizing to one vehicle or a smaller vehicle)

| Description | Monthly Amount |
|---|---|
| Average Monthly Maintenance | $ |
| Monthly Fuel | $ |
| Monthly Loan or Lease Payment | $ |
| Monthly Auto Insurance | $ |
| Auto Taxes, License, Registration (Monthly Cost) | $ |
| Carwash and or Detail | $ |
| Parking Costs | $ |
| | $ |
| | $ |
| **Total Monthly Vehicle Expenses** | **$** |

| Expected Services and Amenity Monthly Expenses (Worksheet B) | |
|---|---|
| **Description** | **Monthly Amount** |
| Gym Membership | $ |
| Golf or Country Club Membership | $ |
| Laundry Services | $ |
| Cleaning / Maid Service | $ |
| | $ |
| | $ |
| **Total Expected Amenity Monthly Expenses:** | **$** |

## Monthly Expenses Cost or Savings After Downsizing

| Expected Services and Amenity Monthly Expenses | |
|---|---|
| **Description** | **Monthly Amount** |
| All Total Current Expenses from Worksheet A | $ |
| Subtract All Total Expenses from Worksheet B | $ |
| **Difference Between the Two Above Figures** | **$** |

If the difference between all current expenses (Worksheet A) and expected expenses (Expected Expenses) is a positive sum, then this is how much you will be saving each month after you downsize.

If the difference between all current expenses (Worksheet A) and expected expenses (Expected Expenses) is a negative sum, then this is how much you more your expenses will cost you after you downsize.

## Downsizing Cash Gain

The following basic worksheet will help you estimate how much if any cash you will gain from downsizing. You can complete this whenever you have the information needed.

## Downsizing Cash Gain Worksheet

| **Additional Cash After Downsizing** Will downsizing put money in your pocket? | |
|---|---|
| Sale of Home Net Equity | $ |
| Selling Belongings Estimate | $ |
| Deposits Refunded | $ |
| **Other (List Below)** | |
| | $ |
| | $ |
| | $ |
| | $ |
| | $ |
| | $ |
| | $ |
| | $ |
| | $ |
| **Total of All Amounts Above (Total Cash)** | $ |
| **Subtract** Estimated Cost of Moving | - $ |
| **Total Net Cash Gain of Downsizing** | $ |

# Section II. Senior Living Options and Downsizing

# 3. Senior Care Communities and Downsizing

*"Always there is life which, rightly lived, implies a divine satisfaction."* – Henry David Thoreau

The 'Why' of your downsizing is important as this will dictate much of the "How' and 'What' you do with your belongings.

For example, if you are moving to a smaller home whether renting or buying there are items you will still need. If you are moving in with family, in addition to unloading items for home care such as lawn and garden tools this might be the time to designate or distribute or make plans for heirlooms and things that you want to give family members or others. If you are downsizing to move into senior community living or a specific type of care facility, there will certain items you might retain depending on what you are allowed to move in and have the space for.

Seniors downsize for many reasons and there are numerous choices for less responsibility, specific health needs, financial reasons and family support.

The following general descriptions of the various group care settings demonstrate some of the basic differences between each one and what possessions you are commonly permitted to keep in the space. You will need to request information regarding their policies for belongings from each facility you are considering.

## Assisted Living or Board and Care Homes

Assisted living communities (or board and car) offer independent living with assistance based on your specific needs. They typically assist with medication management, hygiene, dressing, and meals or the "activities of daily living" or ADLS. Rooms are typically private, and bathrooms might be private or shared.

Generally, these homes are state regulated. States evaluate these homes periodically. The staff records all resident medications, any changes in the residents' health or conditions, and all physician's orders.

Assisted Living Facilities are designed for individuals that are somewhat self-sufficient but need some supervision and assistance. In certain states, the term 'assisted living' or 'assisted living facility' encompasses includes all types of group settings that provide support services. In other states, assisted living facilities are specially licensed and regulated by state law. In these states, assisted living facilities must provide the services and features the state

requires. These facilities generally cater to people that do not need the same level of continuous nursing care that is found in a nursing home. People with Alzheimer's disease, or that need 'dementia care' are often housed in dedicated areas.

Medication management, personal care, bathing, grooming, eating or using the toilet, and is given as needed. Medical staff may be on-site or on call. People live in rooms or apartment-style accommodations. They provide group meals and often, social activities. The monthly charge for assisted living is determined by how much care a person requires and varies widely.

Assisted Living Facilities are generally private apartments with a bedroom, bathroom, small kitchen and living area. Others might have semiprivate sleeping areas and shared bathrooms.

## The Two Assisted Living Categories

The first decision for choosing an assisted living facility is the level of needs for medical assistance. Commonly assisted living residents require some help with medication management. Determine if staff will supervise and dispenses the proper medications. Communities and states vary in requirements for who may do this. Ask questions about who does this and if the person is on-site a minimum of 40 hours a week.

**1. Medical Model Assisted Living:** The medical model provides medical care and support. These are usually

facility type buildings where residents are assigned private or shared rooms that are similar to a nursing home. You might see medication dispensaries or carts and a nursing station.

**2. Social Model Assisted Living Communities:** These communities are typically apartment type buildings. Active lifestyle recreational programs are provided, and some have community dining. Healthcare staff such as a nurse is often available during weekdays.

## Other Assisted Living Types or Models

**Independent Living:** As the description defines, people in these communities do not need any or little assistance with daily living (eating, bathing, dressing, bathroom, or continence). These facilities commonly offer one hour of basic daily assistance.

The facilities are often similar to apartments with kitchens and bathrooms. Staff usually provides only minimal supervision.

Recreational and social activities and group transportation to events are sometimes included. A community meal center is also available at some independent living facilities.

**Traditional Assisted Living Facilities:** These are popular in the Unites States and are basically small studio, one bedroom or two-bedroom apartments. Some apartments may be shared by roommates or couples. Meals, activities, and transportation are often available or provided.

Some residents have daily activity needs. A medical evaluation is often part of the application process. Specific support services are billed in addition to any monthly rent.

**Memory Assisted Living:** For individuals with memory issues, Alzheimer's and dementia, people reside in private or shared rooms with 24-hour supervision. This can be in a separate and secure area within a community or a dedicated facility. Activities for memory afflictions such as music, art, and song therapy are frequently available. Costs are more for memory impaired care.

## Services and Costs

Assisted living retirement communities typically provide:

- Three meals per day and sometimes snacks.
- On and off-site social activities.
- Transportation for medical and dental appointments.

Assisted Living or Board and Care Homes commonly provide:

- Unit and community space maintenance.
- Utilities, except the phone and sometimes Wi-Fi.
- Cognitive impairment care.
- Housekeeping one time per week; Linen service as needed;
- 24-7 staff.
- On site nurse usually at least during business hours.
- Incontinence care.

- Emergency call system.

Some of these services may or may not be included in the monthly fee. Costs and services greatly vary between communities. The majority have a base monthly rate and specific care services are added.

Most base rates include room and meals for a fairly independent senior. Additional support and care will be charged for based on the specific care, a package price, or sometimes a point system.

The base rate usually does not include:
- Shower assistance
- Dressing and grooming assistance
- Medication management
- Other personal services

## *Get Full Disclosure of Costs*

Assisted living communities are required by law to provide you with a written disclosure of the care service they offer. Admitting anyone they cannot care for is illegal.

At each facility you visit, request all full costs. Compare costs between 'all-inclusive rate' communities and 'base rates plus services' communities. Frequently an all-inclusive rate community can be more economical when additional services are needed.

## *Veterans*

If you or your spouse is a veteran, you might qualify for VA benefits under the Aid and Attendance Program/VA. There are specific financial and health requirements.

If you need help with your daily activities, or you're housebound, you may qualify for Aid and Attendance or Housebound allowances in addition to your pension benefits. Find out if you can get these monthly payments added to the amount of your monthly pension.

Finding out if you qualify is a free service. You may qualify for Aid and Attendance if you get a VA pension and you meet at least one of the requirements listed below.

At least one of these must be true:
- You need another person to help you perform daily activities, like bathing, feeding, and dressing, or
- You have to stay in bed—or spend a large portion of the day in bed—because of illness, or
- You are a patient in a nursing home due to the loss of mental or physical abilities related to a disability, or
- Your eyesight is limited (even with glasses or contact lenses you have only 5/200 or less in both eyes; or concentric contraction of the visual field to 5 degrees or less)

You may qualify for Housebound benefits if you get a VA pension and you spend most of your time in your home because of a permanent disability (a disability that doesn't

go away). Note: You can't get Aid and Attendance benefits and Housebound benefits at the same time.

Who's covered:

- Qualified Veterans
- Qualified surviving spouses

There are 2 ways you can get this benefit:

1. Write to your Pension Management Center (PMC) You can write to the PMC for your state.

Include this information:

Evidence, like a doctor's report, that shows you need Aid and Attendance or Housebound care, or VA Form 21-2680 (Examination for Housebound Status or Permanent Need for Regular Aid and Attendance), which your doctor can fill out.

Download VA Form 21-2680.

Details about what you normally do during the day and how you get places. Details that help show what kind of illness, injury, or mental or physical disability affects your ability to do things, like take a bath, on your own

2. Apply in person; You can bring your information to a VA regional benefit office near you.

## What to Take to Assisted Living

**Cleaning Supplies:** While housekeeping is included in many assisted living facilities, you might still want to clean specific items, take care of a spill, or bring cleanliness up

to your standards. Keeping your own broom, mop, window cleaner, general purpose cleaner and paper towels around can come in handy.

**Personal Décor:** Surrounding yourself with a few personal items such as artwork, photos, decorative pieces, and houseplants can make your new place feel like home. While window coverings are commonly in place, your own curtains could make things feel familiar also.

**Kitchen Housewares:** If meals are provided you might want to have a few dishes, silverware and cooking utensils and pots and pans if you plan on cooking occasionally. Check the facility policy on preparing food in your room or space. If there is no microwave or refrigerator supplied, you might want to add these to your list to keep. A mini fridge might be all you need. If not included, you will need your own trash can.

**Furniture:** Beds are always furnished in assisted living situations. Decide on the size of the bed based on the space available. A twin, double, or full-sized bed is usually all you will need. You will want plenty of room to safely get in and out of the bed and to change the sheets.

Your own bed, chairs and perhaps a sofa that fits in your space will help you feel like home. Limit heavy items and large pieces.

**Personal Items and Toiletries:** You will need your own soaps and shampoos, toothpaste, toothbrush, and mouthwash, hairbrush and comb, shaving items and make-up. Include any denture products, incontinence

supplies, contacts, glasses, medication and hearing aids on this list.

**Clothes:** After the essentials such as pajamas, socks, underwear, and shoes choose your wardrobe based on activities, weather, and space. Be sure to bring clothes hangers and any plastic storage boxes needed.

Keep in mind that commercial laundry machines can be tough on many fabrics. However, limit clothing that will need to go out for dry cleaning.

**Bathroom Items:** You might want a bathroom scale, a waste can, and your own towels and washrags. Find out how often housekeeping will do laundry, if that is included, and base the number of towels and washrags you will need in between. If the shower requires a curtain you might need to bring a shower curtain and rings.

**Bedding:** While housekeeping might be doing the laundry, in most assisted living communities you will need your own sheets, blankets, pillows, pillow cases, and bed spreads. Three sets is usually sufficient. You might want to include your own hamper or laundry basket.

## Other Senior Living Options

There are numerous other living options for seniors based on care required. Most of the following options will provide a bed and minimal furniture if appropriate. Some supply all bedding and most provide all meals. You will need to ask each one that you are considering what other items you can bring and will need.

## Board and Care Homes

Board and care homes are private and in residential settings. A board and care home can be a converted single-family home, duplex or apartment. These homes generally provide a room, meals, and living assistance. There is often a manager in place that helps with arranging for transportation, medications, and daily checks for wellbeing.

## Adult Foster Care Homes

An adult foster care home offers a room and support services usually in a family setting. Foster care is for adults that need occasional or routine assistance with daily living. There is commonly more support in foster care than in a board and care home. There are adult foster care homes that have more complex care available with staff or visiting nurses.

## Residential Care Facility (RCF)

A residential care facility is a group residence sometimes referred to as a board and care home or adult foster home. Rooms can be private or shared. The support is for meals, medication, bathing, dressing, eating, bathroom and care for people who cannot be left alone but do not necessitate skilled nursing care. Residential care facilities commonly also provide socialization and recreational activities.

## Intermediate Care Facility (ICF)

This ICF provides 24-hour care for people that need help with bathing, grooming, toilet and mobility. This is a choice for those seniors that cannot live independently. While skilled nursing is usually available, it is not staffed 23 hours a day with a nurse. That would be the next step up in care or a 'Skilled Nursing Facility'.

## Skilled Nursing Facility (SNF)

A Skilled Nursing Facility or SNF is also referred to as a nursing home. There are nursing services available 24 hours a day for personal and medical care including administration of injections, blood pressure monitoring, managing ventilators and intravenous feedings. Medicaid or Medi-Cal in California might help with costs if you qualify.

## What to Take to an Intermediate Care or Skilled Nursing Facility

When you are downsizing to an intermediate care or skilled nursing facility you should not need furniture.

## The Eden (or Greenhouse) Alternative

The Eden Alternative is a program implemented by certain nursing facilities with the goal of a less institutional environment and more home like. They encourage independence and interaction for residents and contact with plants, animals and children.

## Continuing Care Retirement Communities (CCRCs)

CCRCs provide higher levels of care. A continuing care retirement community offers wide-ranging services including housing and nursing care. CCRCs require contracts that specify the services that will be provided and at what costs. These housing communities are often campus like settings. Residents are assigned housing based on their needs and desires. Care can graduate as per a resident's needs. So, while you might move in living independently if daily care becomes compulsory, you can move to an assisted living section. Some CCRCs require a sizeable upfront payment before moving in.

## Long Term Care

Long-term care is a description of a range of services and supports you might need to meet your personal care needs. Most long-term care is not medical care, but rather assistance with the basic personal tasks of everyday life, or the Activities of Daily Living (ADLs), such as:

- Bathing
- Dressing
- Using the toilet
- Transferring (to or from bed or chair)
- Caring for incontinence
- Eating

Other common long-term care services and supports are assistance with everyday tasks, sometimes called Instrumental Activities of Daily Living (IADLs) including:

- Housework
- Managing money
- Taking medication
- Preparing and cleaning up after meals
- Shopping for groceries or clothes
- Using the telephone or other communication devices
- Caring for pets
- Responding to emergency alerts such as fire alarms

According to LongTermCare.gov the national average costs for long-term care in the United States as of 2017 are:

- $225 a day or $6,844 per month for a semi-private room in a nursing home
- $253 a day or $7,698 per month for a private room in a nursing home
- $119 a day or $3,628 per month for care in an
- assisted living facility (for a one-bedroom unit)
- $20.50 an hour for a health aide
- $20 an hour for homemaker services
- $68 per day for services in an adult day health care center

The cost of long-term care depends on the type and duration of care you need, the provider you use, and where you live. Costs can be affected by certain factors, such as:

- Time of day. Home health and home care services, provided in two-to-four-hour blocks of time referred to as "visits," are generally more expensive in the evening, on weekends, and on holidays
- Extra charges for services provided beyond the basic room, food and housekeeping charges at facilities, although some may have "all inclusive" fees.
- Variable rates in some community programs, such as adult day service, are provided at a per-day rate, but can be more based on extra events and activities

Most long-term care is provided at home. Other kinds of long-term care services and supports are provided by community service organizations and in long-term care facilities. Examples of home care services include:
- An unpaid caregiver who may be a family member or friend
- A nurse, home health or home care aide, and/or therapist who comes to the home

Community support services include:
- Adult day care service centers

- Transportation services
- Home care agencies that provide services on a daily basis or as needed

Often these services supplement the care you receive at home or provide time off for your family caregivers.

Outside the home, a variety of facility-based programs offer more options:

- Nursing homes provide the most comprehensive range of services, including nursing care and 24-hour supervision
- Other facility-based choices include assisted living, board and care homes, and continuing care retirement communities. With these providers, the level of choice over who delivers your care varies by the type of facility. You may not get to choose who will deliver services, and you may have limited say in when they arrive.

**Participant Directed Services** are a way to provide services that lets you control what services you receive, who provides them, and how and when those services are delivered. They provide you with information and assistance to choose and plan for the services and supports that work best for you including:

- Name who you want to provide your services; (can include family and friends).
- Whether you want to use a home care service agency

In facility-based services you generally don't have the option to hire someone independently, but you should have choices about:

- Which staff members provide your care
- The schedule you keep
- The meals you eat

In home and community-based settings, you should have the ability to participate or direct the development of a service plan, provide feedback on services and activities, and request changes as needed.

## Veteran's Communities

There are Veteran's Communities in some states. These offer different levels of care starting with independent living with supportive health and social services, to complete skilled nursing facilities.

## Visiting Facilities

When you have narrowed your choices visit each facility and ask if there are any restrictions on items you may bring. Talk to residents and their family members whenever possible and visit or view living spaces. In addition, make sure the community is clean, smells nice and that staff is engaging with residents in a friendly and professional manner.

# Section III. Downsizing and Moving in with Family

## 4. Family Considerations

*"The child may soon stand face to face with the best father."*
- Henry David Thoreau

### Moving in with Family Forms

| Completed | This chapter contains the following checklists, forms, questionnaires, and or worksheets: |
|---|---|
| ✓ | |
| | Practical and Lifestyle: What to Ask Yourself Before Moving in with Your Family |
| | Practical and Lifestyle Questionnaire for Host Family Members |
| | Family Living Space Questionnaire |
| | Safety, Disability and or Mobility Considerations Questionnaire |

This section will help you evaluate your option to move in with family. The questionnaires and forms also aid in addressing concerns of everyone involved and establishing parameters to help make your experience joyful and organized.

Moving in with family can be an opportunity to bond in a multigenerational experience. Having family around can help you avoid the depression that can come with isolation, receive aid with daily living, and keep a watch out for changes in your health needs.

However due to family dynamics and history, finances, personalities and unresolved issues, without planning this can be the recipe for disaster.

Asking questions and addressing issues before moving in can help make the transition go smoother and enrich the living experience. The following forms and worksheets have been designed to help you and your family consider issues and items and help you plan.

- Practical and Lifestyle Aspects
- Living Space
- Relationships
- Financial Considerations
- Preparation Costs
- Living Expenses

## Practical and Lifestyle Aspects of Moving in With Family

This category includes the practical considerations of moving in with family members. For example:

**Would you be relocating to a new town, city or even climate?** Relocating to a different town or state will require you to acclimate to new surroundings, locate services such as the local pharmacy, doctors, bank, grocery

stores, faith related community, senior facilities, the library, recreation center and others. There might also be adult day care centers, meals, counseling and therapeutic activities in the area.

## Will you need to arrange any in home services?

If respite care, a care giver or home health professional is needed these services should be arranged beforehand or soon after moving in. Establish who pays for these services and how.

## Will you have your own transportation?

You might still drive and will have a vehicle that needs parking. Otherwise you can become dependent on family members for rides or will need to check out local transportation

## Will your social life be disrupted?

If you are moving far you will want to establish a social network in your family's community. This can include joining local organizations and or finding a church or faith-based community.

## Practical and Lifestyle Aspects: What to Ask Yourself Before Moving in with Your Family

| Yes/No | Questions to Ask Yourself |
|---|---|
| | Does moving in with my family require me to relocate a long distance from my current home? |
| | Will I be moving to an area with a different climate? <br> If so, how will that affect your daily life and activities? <br><br> _____ <br> _____ <br> _____ <br> _____ <br> _____ |
| | Will moving in with my family change my social life? If so, what will you do to reestablish a social network after I move? <br><br> _____ <br> _____ <br> _____ <br> _____ <br> _____ <br> _____ <br> _____ <br> _____ |

| Yes/No | Questions to Ask Yourself |
|---|---|
| | Will moving in with my family take me away from any activities such as gym recreation, bowling league, exercise, or other clubs and organizations? |
| | If so, list what you can investigate in your new location: |
| | _____ |
| | _____ |
| | _____ |
| | _____ |
| | _____ |
| | _____ |
| | _____ |
| | Will moving in with my family members require me to relocate and take me away from friends or people I love? |
| | If this is the case how can I stay connected with those people? |
| | _____ |
| | _____ |
| | _____ |
| | _____ |
| | _____ |
| | _____ |

| Yes/No | Questions to Ask Yourself |
|--------|---------------------------|
|        | Will moving in with my family change my current mode of transportation? If so, what will you do to replace your form of transportation and keep you from being solely dependent on family members for rides? <br><br> _____ <br> _____ <br> _____ <br> _____ |
|        | Will moving in with my family take away any of my independence? If so will I feel resentful or appreciative? <br><br> _____ <br> _____ |
|        | Does moving in with my family require me to relocate a long distance from my home? |
|        | Will I be moving to an area with a different climate? <br> If so, how will that affect my daily life and activities? <br><br> _____ <br> _____ <br> _____ <br> _____ <br> _____ |

| Yes/No | Questions to Ask Yourself |
|---|---|
| | Will moving in with my family place me in any unfamiliar situations that make me uncomfortable (such as around children, a hectic environment, constantly meeting new people, etc.)? <br><br> _____ <br> _____ <br> _____ <br> _____ |
| | Will I be moving any pets in with me? <br> What special considerations for my pets are needed? <br><br> _____ <br> _____ <br> _____ |
| | Do I expect to be happy living with my family members? <br> If not, why? <br><br> _____ <br> _____ <br> _____ <br> _____ <br><br> How can I resolve this and be happy? <br><br> _____ <br> _____ |

| Yes/No | Questions to Ask Yourself |
|---|---|
| | **Meal Planning** |
| | Do you have specific foods you eat or a special diet? |
| | _____ |
| | _____ |
| | _____ |
| | Who will prepare meals, and will you eat with family? |
| | _____ |
| | _____ |
| | _____ |
| | Does my food take longer to prepare than the food my family generally eats? |
| | _____ |
| | _____ |
| | _____ |
| | Who will pay for food? |
| | _____ |
| | _____ |
| | _____ |
| | Does my family have all the utensils and kitchen appliances need to prepare my food? If not do I have what is needed? |
| | _____ |
| | _____ |

## Practical and Lifestyle Questionnaire for Host Family Members

| Yes/No | Living with Family: Lifestyle *Questions for Family or Host* |
|---|---|
|  | Does anyone smoke tobacco or marijuana? <br><br> If so, are there specific smoking rules and what are they? <br><br> _____ <br> _____ <br> _____ <br> _____ |
|  | Does anyone involved have a pet or pets? |
|  | If there are pets are those pets safe for everyone that will be living in the home and any visitors? |
|  | Who is responsible for which pets? <br><br> _____ <br> _____ <br> _____ <br> _____ <br> _____ |
|  | Who will be allowed to feed the pet(s)? <br><br> _____ <br> _____ <br> _____ |

| Yes/No | Living with Family: Lifestyle *Questions for Family or Host* |
|---|---|
| | What are the specific parameters for the pets(s)? _____ _____ _____ _____ _____ |
| | Will your (father, mother, relative) be permitted or advised not to answer the door when no one else is home? |
| | Do you have an alarm system? |
| | If you have an alarm system will your (father, mother, relative) and or any required health care helpers be given the code and password? If so, keep a list of anyone this is given to. Change the code and password when any caregiver quits, is terminated or is no longer needed. |
| | What keys will your (father, mother, relative) need? _____ _____ _____ |

| Yes/No | Living with Family: Lifestyle<br>*Questions for Family or Host* |
|---|---|
| | Are there any areas that will be considered off limits for your (father, mother, relative)?<br><br>_____<br>_____<br>_____ |
| | Does your relative have a vehicle they will be bringing? |
| | Where will this vehicle be parked?<br><br>_____<br>_____ |
| | Are there parameters for visitors?<br>Is so what are they?<br><br>_____<br>_____<br>_____<br>_____ |
| | Does your relative own any firearms? |
| | Will your relative be allowed to possess or have access to any firearms in your home? |
| | Are there any tools, appliances etc. that your parent or relative will not be allowed to use?<br><br>_____<br>_____ |

| Yes/No | Living with Family: Lifestyle<br>*Questions for Family or Host* |
|---|---|
| | Meal Planning<br>Does your parent or relative require specific foods or a special diet?<br><br>_____<br>_____<br>_____<br>_____<br>_____ |
| | Who will prepare meals?<br><br>_____<br>_____<br>_____<br>_____<br>_____ |
| | Will your family members eat together or at the same times as your parent or relative?<br><br>_____<br>_____<br>_____<br>_____ |
| | Who will pay for food?<br><br>_____<br>_____<br>_____ |

## Living Space

Moving in with other family members will require planning. In addition to the space requirements there might also be special needs for mobility or vision issues for example. Seniors can require special adaptations. Some of these changes are not expensive but will require time and planning for installation.

This section is mostly for host families or household members.

Consider where your parent/relative will stay in your home and if anyone will be displaced from their room or inconvenienced. If needed and within your budget, consider a room addition.

Some home health agencies will perform home evaluations for senior and special needs living for safety and mobility. Evaluate the available space for privacy and mobility and avoid stairs when possible. See the lists at the end of this section for more considerations.

## Moving

When moving a parent into your home, he or she will have clothing, personal items, and depending on the length of stay expected and space available maybe furniture and personal items.

This is often the time your parent or relative will need to downsize their belongings.

## Privacy

Privacy is a consideration for your family and your relative that will move in. This includes bedroom and bathroom privacy and possibly a private entrance to the area. If caregivers are entering your home, you and your family will want to maintain your privacy with these people also.

You might need to declare certain areas off limits and even install interior door locks for those rooms, especially if your relative has any cognitive challenges that might cause him or her to wander or become disoriented.

## Home Prepping

To prepare your home for a senior relative, consider their needs for:

- space
- privacy
- safety
- living accommodations

Stairs – If your relative has any challenge with stairs, consider an electric stair lift. While they are expensive, they can be less than the cost of adding a room on a first floor if none is available.

The chair lifts provide a safe alternative to staircases. The lifts are electric motorized chairs that attaches to a rail that still allows use of the chairs by other household members.

Otherwise make stairs as safe as possible with no slip surfaces or low pile carpeting, nightlights, and a strong bannister or handrail.

## Bedroom

Your relative should have a private bedroom that provides enough space belongings, wardrobe, and any needed safety, mobility, and health equipment needed.

Bed height is another important factor for seniors and mobility. When knees are higher than hips while in a sitting position on the edge of the bed, the bed height is too low. If feet are not touching the floor the bed height is too high.

## Bathroom

The bathroom should be close to your relative's bedroom and on the same floor. Use non-slip mats on bathroom floors and if needed in bathtubs and showers. Taller commodes are available and appreciated by most seniors. There are also lids with removable arms.

Consider installing a walk-in tub. Add a stool for seating and install safety rails near the commode and in the shower or bathtub. There are safety rails that can double as towel bars. Towel bars are not designed for people to stable themselves or prevent a fall. Consider replacing them with secured safety bars.

## Clutter

Provide adequate storage and organizational space for your

relative's belongings to help them stay clutter free. Realize they might need some assistance to stay organized.

## Emergency Intercom

Installing an emergency intercom in your guest's bedroom so they can alert you if needed is a great idea. Your

## Nightlights

Keep hallways, bathrooms, and doorways illuminated with nightlights.

## Electrical Cords

Electrical cords can be a trip and fall hazard. Tape cords down if needed and run them out of the way behind furniture.

## Medication

Store medications in a daily pill organizer in the bathroom, bedroom, or kitchen.  Make sure all medication is labeled and kept out of reach and secured from accessibility by children.

## Living Areas

Like beds, chairs should be the right height. You can add cushions to raise seat height when needed. Make sure all chairs and other furniture is secure and not wobbly. Remove throw rugs and check all thresholds for hazards.

## Lighting

Lights need to illuminate enough and be working. Add more floor or ceiling light if needed. Install the 'Clapper' in areas such as the bedroom so the senior can get into bed

with the light on and then shut the light out. Use motion-sensor lights outdoors for entry and exits areas.

### Railings and Banisters

Make sure secure railings and bannisters are installed in stairways, bathrooms and anywhere else needed. All steps and stairways should always be well lit.

### Kitchen

Keep items that your relative will use within their reach.

### Tools

Keep tools and chemicals in a secure place. If your relative has dementia these items can cause injury.

### Outside

If your parent or loved one is at risk for wandering keep doors closed and locked and install alarms. You can also investigate a Bluetooth tracking device if the situation warrants.

Complete the following 'Safety, Disability and or Mobility Considerations Questionnaire'.

**Note:** For estimating the costs of home prepping, there is a 'Home Preparation Costs Planning Form' in the 'Financial Considerations' section found later in this chapter.

## Living with Family: Space Questionnaire

| Yes/No | Living with Family: Living Space |
|--------|----------------------------------|
| | *Questions for Host Person or Family* |
| | Will you have a local home health agency perform a home evaluation of your home prior to having your relative move in? <br><br> _____ <br><br> _____ |
| | Do you have room in your home to provide the privacy your parent or relative is comfortable with, and to maintain your family's privacy? |
| | Do you have a private bathroom for your new resident? |
| | Is there a separate entrance for your relative? |
| | Who will provide the needed furniture? |
| | Will your home accommodations be sufficient for the next one to three years? |
| | Is any remodeling required to build accommodations such as a bedroom, bathroom or private entrance? <br><br> If the answer is 'yes' who will pay for this and how? <br><br> _____ <br><br> _____ <br><br> _____ |

| Yes/No | Living with Family: Living Space |
|---|---|
| | *Questions for Host Person or Family* |
| | How long is any remodeling expected to take until complete? <br><br> _____ <br><br> Expected Completion Date: <br><br> _____ <br><br> Expected Move-In Date is <br><br> _____ |
| | What is the estimated cost of the move and who will pay for this? |
| | Will a storage unit be needed to move any of your belongings out of your home to make room? |
| | Notes: |
| | |
| | |
| | |
| | |
| | |
| | |

## Safety, Disability and or Mobility Considerations Questionnaire

| Yes or No | Living with Family: Safety, Disability and or Mobility Considerations |
|---|---|
| | *Questions for Host Person or Family* |
| | Does your new resident need to and is he or she capable of navigating steps or stairs safely? |
| | Can your (father, mother, relative) easily and safely 'lock and unlock' and 'open and close' all doors in your home? |
| | Can your (father, mother, relative) easily navigate and exit your home in an emergency from any location? |
| | Can your (father, mother, relative) easily reach all interior and exterior light switches, door handles, locks, and faucets in your home? |
| | Can your (father, mother, relative) smell natural gas? |
| | Can your (father, mother, relative) feel when water is too hot? |
| | Can your (father, mother, relative) hear all alarms, alerts, doorbells, and phones in your home? |
| | Will an emergency intercom be installed? |

| Yes or No | Living with Family: Safety, Disability and or Mobility Considerations |
|---|---|
| | *Questions for Host Person or Family* |
| | Will a third-party emergency alert system be used? |
| | Will your relative be able to control the temperature in his or her space? |
| | If your (father, mother, relative) needs a walker or wheelchair is your home completely accessible? |
| | Will your (father, mother, relative) be permitted to set any temperature controls and if so, can he or she read, reach, and adjust all temperature controls? |
| | Will areas need to be wheelchair accessible? <br><br> _____ <br> _____ <br> _____ |
| | Do any different door handles need to be installed? |
| | Will handrails for assistance be installed in the bathroom? Near commode and in shower area. <br><br> _____ <br> _____ <br> _____ <br> _____ |

| Yes or No | Living with Family: Safety, Disability and or Mobility Considerations |
|---|---|
| | *Questions for Host Person or Family* |
| | Are handrails needed anywhere else in the home such as entry and exit areas? If so where? <br><br> _____ <br> _____ <br> _____ <br> _____ <br> _____ |
| | Hall and Doorway Wheelchair Clearance <br> Will any halls or doorways need to be widened for wheelchair (or walker) clearance? |
| | Will special locks, door chimes and or other alert and prevention devices be installed? |
| | Auto Shut Offs for Stove Tops, Coffee Makers, etc. |
| | Interior and Exterior Lighting |
| | Are laundry facilities easily accessible? |
| | Hazard Review: Dangling Cords, Poisons, Slippery Surfaces, Unsteady Chairs, Throw Rugs, Electrical Cords, etc. |
| | Hot Water Maximum Temperature Set to 120 Degrees F |

| Yes or No | Living with Family: Safety, Disability and or Mobility Considerations |
| --- | --- |
| | *Questions for Host Person or Family* |
| | Is the bed height correct? When the senior's knees are higher than hips while in a sitting position on the edge of the bed, the bed height is too low. If feet are not touching the floor the bed height is too high. |
| | Will a raised toilet seats or taller commode be installed? When the senior's knees are higher than hips while in a sitting position, the commode height is too low. If feet are not touching the floor the height is too high. |

# 5. Financial Considerations

*"Goodness is the only investment that never fails."*
– Henry David Thoreau

## Moving in with Family
## Financial Considerations Forms

| Completed ✓ | This chapter contains the following forms; |
|---|---|
|  | Home Preparation Costs Planning Form |
|  | Living Expenses Planning Form |

## Financial Considerations for Your Family

Having an elderly relative move into your home can require renovation costs and added daily living expenses. Depending on your parent's mobility and other needs, you might have to install safety features and even add or remodel rooms. These costs can add up fast.

If a walker or wheelchair is required, doorways need to be at least 36 inches wide, some furniture might need to be relocated or removed, ramps installed, and door handles made lower.

If you or a family member leave a job or reduce work hours to take care of your elderly relative, there might be a

significant loss of income. In this case, some people change to telecommuting or start a job or other income they can produce from home.

Other financial factors will depend on your parent's specific situation. At this time, social security benefits will be reduced by one third if you are not paying your children of family members any rent. SSI deems free room and board as 'in-kind support and maintenance.'

There are also daily living expenses, transportation, and health costs. AARP reports that the average cost of an in-home health aide is more than $20,000 a year.

How Moving in Elderly Parents into Your Home Can Affect Your Taxes

Tax law is perpetually changing so you should consult with your accountant or tax preparer for current information. As of this writing, here are a few ways your tax liability could be affected:

As of this writing, if you claim your elderly parent as a dependent, his or her income limitation is $3,950 a year (not including social security payments). In order to qualify as a dependent, you must also have paid more than 50% of your parent's expenses for the year.

There might also be qualifying tax deductions for money you pay for dentures, hearing aids, wheel chairs, walkers, medical transportation and increased utility bills and grocery expense.

See IRS Publication 501 for regulations about dependents.

In the case where your parent pays you rent, you need to declare that as income on Schedule E.

### Insurance

Because health and medical care can be costly for seniors, if you are moving in with your adult children you will need to discuss your insurance coverage. As with all subjects regarding moving in, express your fears and expectations and discuss your finances. While this might be awkward at first, this can open the door to easier conversations and mutually beneficial solutions.

## Home Preparation Costs Planning Form

| Description | Amount |
|---|---|
| Room Addition | $ |
| Remodeling | $ |
| Bathroom Addition | $ |
| Bathroom Fixtures / Handrails | $ |
| Bathroom Accessories | $ |
| Stair or Hallway Handrails | $ |
| Stair Chair Lift | $ |

| Description | Amount |
|---|---|
| Moving or changing interior and exterior light switches door handles, locks, and faucets in your home | $ |
| Moving or changing Door Handles / Locks | $ |
| Moving or changing faucets | $ |
| Installing any intercom, alarms or systems | $ |

71

| Description | Amount |
|---|---|
| Interior or Exterior Lighting Installations or Changes <br><br> _____ <br> _____ <br> _____ <br> _____ | $ |
| Wheelchair Accessible Remodeling <br><br> _____ <br> _____ <br> _____ <br> _____ <br> _____ | $ |
| Wheelchair Ramps <br><br> _____ <br> _____ <br> _____ <br> _____ | $ |
| Interior and Exterior Lighting Installations or Changes <br><br> _____ <br> _____ <br> _____ <br> _____ | $ |
| Total Estimated Home Preparation Costs | $ |

## Living Expenses

Living expenses include food costs, personal hygiene items, transportation, possible utility cost increases and any other daily living costs. Medical or assistance expenses include those covered by insurance and services that are not covered such as a home caregiver.

- You will need to make decisions such as:
- Who will pay for your guest's food?
- What transportation will you need to provide?
- Will you need to buy your guest personal hygiene items?
- Will your parent or relative require in home care?
- Will you or a spouse need to reduce work hours or quit a job to care for your parent or relative?
- Can you afford the extra expenses?
- Will anyone else (such as a sibling) contribute to expenses?

Write down and express your expectations about care, chores, meals, and any other costs. Moving your parent or relative is not always only about finances, however, be aware that expenses are commonly more than anticipated.

## Living with Family Monthly Expenses Worksheet (for Families)

| Living with Family Monthly Expenses Worksheet Questions for Your Family |
| --- |
| **Meals and Diet** |
| Does your family member have special diet requirements and if so, what is the estimated monthly cost of these meals?<br><br>Monthly Cost: $ _____<br><br>Who will pay for this food? _____ |
| Otherwise how much will your family member contribute to groceries monthly?<br><br>Monthly Contribution: $ _____ |
| **Rent** |
| Will your family member be paying rent and if so, how much?<br><br>Monthly Rent: $ _____ |
| **Internet and Phone** |
| Does your family member have his or her own cell phone?<br>Yes \_\_\_\_\_ No \_\_\_\_\_<br><br>Who will pay for this phone? _____ |
| Will your family member have any specific Internet or cable needs?<br>Yes \_\_\_\_\_ No \_\_\_\_\_ Monthly Cost $ _____ |

## Living with Family Monthly Expenses Worksheet Questions for Your Family

### Transportation

How many times on average each week does your family member need to go somewhere that requires transportation?

_____

_____

_____

_____

Does your family member have his or her own vehicle and driver's license?  Yes _____  No _____

If 'Yes' who will pay for gas, car maintenance, and insurance?

_____

_____

_____

If 'Yes' is easily accessible parking available for your family member's vehicle?  Yes _____  No _____

If 'No' what forms of transportation will be available?

_____

_____

_____

_____

_____

## Living with Family Financial Worksheet
## Questions for Your Family

### Utilities

Will your family member need any additional utility services or increase your utility usage and cost in any way?

If so, how much for each monthly?

Utility _____ Monthly Amount $_____

Utility _____ Monthly Amount $_____

Utility _____ Monthly Amount $_____

Utility _____ Monthly Amount $_____

Utility _____ Monthly Amount $_____

Total Monthly    $_____

Will your family member need to hire help in the form of home care, nursing, or aid?   Yes _____ No _____

If Yes: Estimated Monthly Cost:

_____

Who will pay for this care?

_____

_____

Will having my parent (or relative) move into my home increase my monthly expenses?

# 6. Family Relationships

*"Ignorance and bungling with love are better than wisdom and skill without."* – Henry David Thoreau

### Moving in with Family Forms

| Completed ✓ | This chapter contains the following forms and worksheets: |
|---|---|
| | Living with Family Relationship Worksheet for You |
| | Living with Family Relationship Worksheet for Your Family |
| | Household Rules for Living with Family Form |

When you live with people that you haven't lived with in decades, old patterns of behavior can show up. If you and your parent used to fight about a household issue, that might come up again. Or if one of your siblings is around more to help with your parent, you might find yourself revisiting childhood fights. Simply being aware of these patterns can help you avoid them and defuse the situation. Meeting with a professional that specializes in family relationships can help.

**For adult children having a parent (s) move into their home:**

Set ground rules and expectations for you, your family and your parent. Recognize that your parent is giving up some independence and that you might well be in the same situation one day. Think about how you would feel and empathize.

Assure your parent that you will not tell him or her what to do or criticize. When your parent expresses a concern, listen and repeat the concern back to your parent to be sure you understand.

Avoid discussions of politics, values or belief systems if you do not agree.

Make everyone's privacy a priority with clear boundaries.

If you have children living in your home set a positive tone with them from the start.

Sometimes a senior's behavior can scare or even embarrass children. Especially if the senior is suffering from health issues' Tell your children they are not to blame for and of your relative's (or their grandparent's) potential behavior.

## Living with Family Relationship Worksheet for You

| Yes/No | Questions to Ask Yourself Before Moving In |
|---|---|
| | Will moving in with my family reduce my monthly expenses? |
| | Will I have the privacy I need? |
| | Does my family have a healthy way of addressing conflicts? |
| | Do I enjoy spending long periods of time with my family? |
| | |
| | Are there unresolved issues between my family and me or between other family members that could interfere with peacefully living with my family? <br><br> _____ <br> _____ <br> _____ |
| | Are all parties willing to work to resolve these issues? <br> How can these issues be resolved? <br><br> _____ <br> _____ <br> _____ <br> _____ |

| Yes/No | Questions to Ask Yourself Before Moving In |
|---|---|
| | Is there any pattern of personality conflict between my any family members and me? |
| | If the answer is 'Yes' are there 'triggers' or specific things that set these conflicts off?  If so, what are they? <br><br> _____ <br> _____ <br> _____ <br> _____ <br> _____ |
| | What can be done to avoid conflicts with my family? <br><br> _____ <br> _____ <br> _____ <br> _____ |
| | If I disagree with anything my adult child does, am I comfortable discussing it? <br><br> _____ |
| | Am I comfortable with all members of my family including any children or grandchildren? <br><br> _____ <br> _____ <br> _____ |

| Yes/No | Questions to Ask Yourself Before Moving In |
|--------|---------------------------------------------|
|        | If there are children in the home, do I have a preestablished relationship with them? |
|        | Am I allowed to correct the children? |
|        | Are there any conflicts of authority over the children? |
|        | Are the children comfortable with me moving into the home? (if they are not this might need to be addressed with a professional before considering the move.) |
|        | What boundaries would be beneficial to establish?<br><br>_____<br>_____<br>_____<br>_____<br>_____<br>_____<br>_____<br>_____<br>_____<br>_____<br>_____<br>_____<br>_____ |

| Yes/No | Questions to Ask Yourself Before Moving In |
|--------|--------------------------------------------|
|        | What do I expect from each of my family members regarding any type of assistance? <br><br> _____ <br> _____ <br> _____ <br> _____ <br> _____ <br> _____ <br> _____ <br> _____ |
|        | Do I expect my family to provide rides or any transportation services and will I pay them to do this? |
|        | Do my family members ever ask me for money? |
|        | Can my family afford their current lifestyle? |
|        | Will moving in with my family create any financial burden or hardship on them? |
|        | Can I have visitors to the home? If so, are there limitations or boundaries such as who can visit and when? <br><br> _____ <br> _____ <br> _____ |

## Living with Family Relationship Worksheet for Your Family

| Yes/No | Questions Your Family Needs to Ask |
|---|---|
| | Will all family members have the privacy they need? |
| | Do I and my family members enjoy spending long periods of time with my parent? |
| | Are there unresolved issues between my parent and my children? |
| | Does my family have a healthy way of addressing conflicts? |
| | How can these issues be resolved? <br><br> _____ <br> _____ <br> _____ <br> _____ <br> _____ |
| | Are there unresolved issues between my parent and my spouse or any other household residents? |
| | How can these issues be resolved? <br><br> _____ <br> _____ <br> _____ <br> _____ |

| Yes/No | Questions Your Family Needs to Ask |
|---|---|
| | Is there any pattern of personality conflict between my parent and myself or anyone else in the house? |
| | If the answer is 'Yes' are there 'triggers' or specific things that set these conflicts off?  If so, what are they? |
| | _____ _____ _____ _____ _____ |
| | What can be done to avoid these conflicts? |
| | _____ _____ _____ _____ _____ |
| | What boundaries would be beneficial to establish to avoid conflicts? |
| | _____ _____ _____ _____ _____ |

| Yes/No | Questions Your Family Needs to Ask |
|--------|-----------------------------------|
| | If I (we) disagree with my parent, am I comfortable discussing it? |
| | Are all members of the household comfortable with my parent? |
| | Are my children safe and comfortable in the presence of my parent? |
| | Is my parent allowed to correct the children? |
| | Are there any conflicts of authority over the children? |
| | What boundaries would be beneficial to establish with the children? <br><br> _____ <br> _____ <br> _____ <br> _____ <br> _____ |
| | How does my parent feel about moving in? <br><br> _____ <br> _____ <br> _____ |
| | Does my parent expect to attend events with the family or family members and is this OK? |
| | Does my parent expect to go on vacation with the family and is this OK? |

| Yes/No | Questions Your Family Needs to Ask |
|---|---|
| | How do each of my household members feel about my parent moving in? _____ _____ _____ _____ |
| | Does my parent expect me and or my family members to provide him or her with transportation? |
| | If so, is providing transportation OK and under what circumstances? _____ _____ _____ |
| | Will my parent or relative be bringing a pet into the home? Does this pet fit with our lifestyle? Does this pet get along with children and any pets already in the home? Can my parent or relative provide the care for this pet? |
| | Will my parent be expected to babysit (or pet sit) at any time? _____ |

| Yes/No | Questions Your Family Needs to Ask |
|---|---|
| | Does my parent or relative have any special considerations that everyone needs to be aware of such as:<br><br>• reduced cognitive functions<br>• loss of memory<br>• depression<br>• medication effects<br>• challenge with balance or mobility |
| | Are family meals customary? |
| | Does my parent expect to have family meals? |
| | Will any household members need to change their work or school schedules to accommodate my relative?<br><br>If so who and how?<br><br>_____<br>_____<br>_____<br>_____<br><br>Will my household income be affected by changes in work schedules? If so, estimate how much:<br><br>_____<br>_____ |

## Household Rules for Living with Family Form

| House Rules |
| --- |
| What boundaries would be beneficial to establish? |
|  |
|  |
|  |
|  |
|  |
|  |
|  |
|  |
|  |
| Will there be specific assigned responsibilities in the home? |
|  |
|  |
|  |
|  |

## Notes About Living with Family

89

# Section IV. Your Possessions

# 7. Should You Keep Your Vehicle(s)?

*"Simplify your life. Don't burden yourself with possessions. Keep your needs and wants simple and enjoy what you have. Don't destroy your peace of mind by looking back, worrying about the past. Live in the present. Simplify!"*
- Henry David Thoreau

 **Your Vehicle Forms**

| Completed ✓ | This chapter contains the following forms and worksheets: |
|---|---|
| | Selling Your Vehicle Checklist |

The decision to keep or sell your vehicle(s) is based on:

- Ability to drive
- Need to drive
- Desire to drive
- Cost to drive
- Vehicle Parking or Storage Available

Depending on your situation you might not need a vehicle after you downsize. After downsizing some people have

discovered that renting a vehicle periodically or using a taxi service is all they need. If you will be keeping and maintaining a vehicle you might consider downsizing to one vehicle and /or to a smaller vehicle.

## Selling Your Vehicle

If you have decided to sell your vehicle, make sure you do this when you are close to, or after, moving when you no longer need it. You can sell your vehicle by advertising in local newspaper classified ads and online at sites such as Craigslist. Clean your car and take clear digital pictures of your vehicle for online ads.

You can get your vehicle's current value at websites such as:

https://www.kbb.com/whats-my-car-worth/
http://www.nadaguides.com/

**Transaction Safety:** When people want to see my vehicle for sale, I usually meet them with my car at the local police station parking lot (preferably in the view of a security camera). This prevents them from being at my home and offers some assurance of safety. If they want to buy the car I have them follow me to the bank (if the bank is open.) I accept only cash in full for a vehicle at the time of sale; if a check, cashier's check, or money order is fraudulent or has insufficient funds there is little recourse and at best a difficult situation.

In many cases this can be a large sum of money, so I prefer to meet at a bank and do the transaction inside the bank. Then I can immediately deposit the money without risking loss or being the victim of theft.

If you are at all uncomfortable selling your vehicle, enlist the help of a friend or relative.

For more information about aging and driving I recommend *Aging in Suburbia: The Must-Have Conversation About Homes and Driving* by Jane Gould; available on Amazon.

## Selling Your Vehicle Checklist

| DONE | SELLING YOUR VEHICLE ITEM |
|---|---|
| | **Keys:** Gather all keys for your vehicle. |
| | **Contents:** Remove all contents from the vehicle before you sell. This includes your registration and proof of insurance. |
| | **Title:** Have your titled ready but do not sign it until you are making the transaction. |
| | **Bill of Sale:** In some states a bill of sale is also required. Having a bill of sale whether it is required or not where you live is a good idea. |
| | **Emissions:** In some states a recent valid emissions test is required before selling a vehicle. |
| | **License Plate:** Remove your license plates from the vehicle before the sale. Leaving your license plates on the car for the new owner could create liability issues for you. |
| | **Insurance:** Call your insurance agent as soon as possible after you sell your car to cancel the policy. |
| | |
| | |
| | |

# 8. How Can You Downsize Your Wardrobe and Still Have Everything You Need?

 **Wardrobe Forms**

| Completed ✓ | This chapter contains the following checklists and worksheets: |
|---|---|
| | Wardrobe Worksheet |
| | Wardrobe Checklist |

Most of us have more clothing than we need and can downsize our wardrobe. The chief considerations are what clothing do you need based on:

- Seasons of Residence
- Travel
- Space
- Employment
- Lifestyle
- Preferences
- Laundry Availability

Where you will live, and travel contributes to what seasons you need attire for. How you will store your clothing and how much space you have for laundry, and how often you

will do laundry will also help you decide how much clothing to keep.

The wardrobe worksheet will help you evaluate what you need clothing for then you will need to decide what clothing you will keep.

## Wardrobe Worksheet

What seasons do I need clothing for?

___ Spring
___ Summer
___ Fall
___ Winter


How much space will I have for clothing storage?

_____

_____

_____


What type of space will I have for clothing? (Hanging clothes, shelving, drawers, boxes or containers or other)

_____

_____

_____

_____


What storage space will I have for clothes that need laundering?

_____

What laundry facilities will I have and how often will I do laundry?

What are my daily clothes that fit my lifestyle?

Do I need specific clothing for employment?

Do I need formal wear and if so what?

_____

_____

Will I travel frequently and if so, what clothing will I need?

_____

_____

_____

_____

_____

_____

What accessories do I need?  (Jewelry, hair ties, neckties, belts, etc.)

_____

_____

_____

_____

_____

_____

_____

_____

_____

_____

_____

_____

## Sorting Your Clothing

Step 1:  Begin with 3 piles, or large boxes or bags and label them:

- Keep
- Donate
- Discard

Step 2: As you remove each item from your closet or dresser place it in one of the three piles.

3. Find your favorite signature items and accessories (if any). Keep those. Build flexible outfits around items you wear often.

4. Discard clothing if:

- You haven't worn an item in the last 12 months.

- An item is worn or beyond repair.
- An item does not fit you anymore.
- You don't like the item.

In the future keep your clothes in view if possible. When you can see all your clothes, you get a better idea of what you usually wear and don't wear. Put them on shelves, in clear plastic boxes, or organize your closet so that you can see everything. Then clothing does not get hidden away and forgotten behind other items, in bags or in drawers.

## Wardrobe Checklist

| | WARDROBE ITEMS TO KEEP |
|---|---|
| | **Casual** |
| | Jeans |
| | Short Sleeve Shirts |
| | Long Sleeve Shirts |
| | T Shirts |
| | Shorts |
| | Shoes |
| | Socks |
| | Undergarments |
| | Pants |
| | Pajamas |
| | House Coat |
| | |
| | |
| | |
| | |
| | |
| | |
| | |
| | |

| | WARDROBE ITEMS TO KEEP |
|---|---|
| | **Weather Related** |
| | Jackets |
| | Coats |
| | Hats |
| | Gloves |
| | Rain Gear |
| | Boots |
| | |
| | |
| | |
| | |
| | |
| | |
| | |
| | |
| | |
| | |
| | |
| | |
| | |

| | WARDROBE ITEMS TO KEEP |
|---|---|
| | **Formal** |
| | Suits |
| | Dresses |
| | Skirts |
| | Shoes |
| | |
| | |
| | |
| | **Work Attire** |
| | |
| | |
| | |
| | |
| | |
| | |
| | |
| | |
| | |
| | |

| | WARDROBE ITEMS TO KEEP |
|---|---|
| | **Sports or Activity Related** |
| | |
| | |
| | |
| | |
| | |
| | |
| | **Other** |
| | |
| | |
| | |
| | |
| | |
| | |
| | |
| | |

Download all forms in printable format for free here:
http://www.formgal.com/thoreauplanners.htm

# 9. How Can You Downsize Your Stuff?

*"With respect to luxuries and comforts, the wisest have ever lived a more simple and meagre life than the poor."*
– Henry David Thoreau

### Downsize Your Stuff Forms

| Completed ✓ | This chapter contains the following list; |
|---|---|
|  | What to Keep List |

Our relationships with possessions can be complex... it's how and why you buy, then how you say goodbye... and everything in between.

Choosing which items, you will say 'goodbye' to, can be arduous. Some people find parting with certain or any possessions difficult. (I should know!)

Although we already had one that we liked, we received four toasters for wedding presents. I felt like getting rid of any of them would be disrespectful to my marriage. We hauled them from place to place as we moved. Our possessions grew beyond our space and seven years later I

was cleaning out our storage locker and found all four still in the box and damaged.

## The Why of Acquisition

If you are having difficulty deciding what to let go of or just letting go, start by looking at how you purchase or attain an item.

How did you acquire the item?

- Purchase
- Gift
- Inheritance
- Prize
- Free
- Buy with another person

Did you shop and shop to find the item or get a great deal? Sometimes we equate the value of an item with the work and or time involved in the acquisition.

Other items are memory associated. These items can remind us of a happy time, a person, or another memory we want to hold onto.

Ask yourself:

How did you feel when you bought this possession?

For example:

- Was this item a bargain?
- Was this item a big purchase at the time?

- Did you buy the item with family member or friends        present?
- Do you remember the day?

Then ask yourself:

- What does the item represent to you?
- How do you feel about the object?

And one question that has helped me get rid of many of my belongings... 'Would you buy this item today?' Most of the time I have to say no. Out it goes.

Discovering the when, what, who, why, and how of your belongings can help you make better downsizing decisions, change your mind set about acquiring items, and help develop the habits to stay organized.

## How Can Vilfredo's Principle Help You Downsize?

**The Pareto Principle** is derived from economist Vilfredo Pareto. The principle denotes that 80 percent of consequences come from 20 percent of the causes. Pareto observed the relationship between wealth and citizens. He saw that 80 percent of the land in Italy was owned by 20 percent of the population.

Pareto studied a number of other countries and found the ratio was the same. Over time, the Pareto Principle has been found to apply to a great number of inputs and outputs and is often referred to as the '80/20 Rule'.

While not an exact measurement, the 80/20 Rule is a general ratio that also applies to your possessions. If you recorded the total usage of all your possessions as to how often you use them, you will find that generally speaking, you use about 20% of your belongings 80% of the time. The remaining 80% of your possessions you use only about 20% of the total time.

The 20% commonly includes:

- Personal items such as keys, wallet, purse, phone, glasses, coffee cup, slippers, etc.
- Certain bathroom items such as soap (hopefully), toothbrush, mouthwash, razor, etc.
- Kitchen items that are in the 20% include dishes, silver ware, glasses and so on.

**Take Inventory with Purpose**

Rather than just making a list of all your stuff, take inventory of your belongings by using the 'Stuff Lists' in this chapter. You will decide what you are going to do with each item as you go. Then you will be eliminating the step of having to go back and decide what to do with each one.

The stuff lists include:

1. What to Keep List

2. What to Donate or Give Away List

3. What to Sell List

4. What to Throw Away List

5. What to Put in Storage List

6. What to Replace List

Going through a life time of stiff can be overwhelming. Do one room at a time. You can use colored tags or stickers to designate which list each item is on. For example:

**Red:** What to Keep List

**Green:** What to Donate or Give Away List

**White:** What to Sell List

**Orange:** What to Throw Away List

**Blue:** What to Put in Storage List

**Purple:** What to Replace List

'White' is good for the 'What to Sell List' as they can later become 'price tags'. You can price these items if you know what you will want for them as you make your lists if you are planning to sell them in the next 30 days. Otherwise you can price them later.

Consider where each item will go in your new place before you add it to the 'What to Keep' list. This will help you be organized when you get there so you don't end up with a cluttered living space.

**TIP:** You might need new or different furniture after you move. Consider furniture with storage options such as shelving units, coffee or end tables with storage, ottomans with built-in storage, a bed with storage drawers underneath, etc. By being organized and utilizing storage furniture in your smaller living space, you'll feel less cramped in your new home.

As you enter items on the 'What to Give Away or Donate List' decide who they will go to. Don't get stuck on the small stuff such as jewelry, paperwork, and pictures; if you cannot decide if you want to keep an item or not mark it as a keeper for now.

Think in terms of needs with utility type items such as kitchen utensils. If you are moving to a facility that provides meals or in with relatives, you should be able to give away or sell most of these pieces.

Other than dusting off the items themselves, if needed, avoid cleaning as you sort. Generally, the sorting will require your energy and focus. Cleaning is easier later after items have been removed.

For many people this is an easier task with company. An impartial friend can often offer a better perspective than family members such as those you will be giving items to.

If you have the time, you might dedicate a few hours a day to this task when you are rested and less likely to be interrupted. Sorting through your history can bring up memories and be draining. If you become overwhelmed take a break.

If you have grown children now is the time for them to claim their keepsakes such as trophies, awards, CDs, pictures, posters, school papers, etc.

*"The memory of some past moments is more persuasive than the experience of present ones."* – Henry David Thoreau

**TIP:** If you are attached to certain items that have sentimental value that you are giving away, take pictures of them. You can create a virtual or scrap book of these items so that you can 'visit' them whenever you wish.

## Kitchen

*"He who distinguishes the true savor of his food can never be a glutton; he who does not cannot be otherwise."* — Henry David Thoreau

What kitchen items you will need to keep depend on where you are going. If you are moving into a smaller home or from a home to an apartment, or into a group setting, for example, you will still need kitchen items. If you are relocating to a facility where meals will be prepared for you, obviously you will not require many or maybe any kitchen appliances or items.

When downsizing, you will probably not be entertaining large groups of people, so you can discard or sell extra

table ware and glasses. Don't keep duplicate items that you could only possibly need in rare situations, and limit possessions to what will be commonly used.

## Garage and Tools

If you will no longer be taking care of any outdoor maintenance or a yard, you will be able to sell, give away, or discard your gardening and lawn maintenance tools. You might need to keep a few tools such as a power drill for hanging items in your new residence.

Be sure to dispose of any flammable or hazardous materials properly (see the chapter 'Discarding Stuff').

## What to Keep List

| PACKED | ITEM TO KEEP | LOCATION |
|--------|--------------|----------|
|  |  |  |
|  |  |  |
|  |  |  |
|  |  |  |
|  |  |  |
|  |  |  |
|  |  |  |
|  |  |  |
|  |  |  |
|  |  |  |
|  |  |  |
|  |  |  |
|  |  |  |
|  |  |  |
|  |  |  |

| PACKED | ITEM TO KEEP | LOCATION |
|--------|--------------|----------|
|        |              |          |
|        |              |          |
|        |              |          |
|        |              |          |
|        |              |          |
|        |              |          |
|        |              |          |
|        |              |          |
|        |              |          |
|        |              |          |
|        |              |          |
|        |              |          |
|        |              |          |
|        |              |          |
|        |              |          |

| PACKED | ITEM TO KEEP | LOCATION |
|--------|--------------|----------|
|        |              |          |
|        |              |          |
|        |              |          |
|        |              |          |
|        |              |          |
|        |              |          |
|        |              |          |
|        |              |          |
|        |              |          |
|        |              |          |
|        |              |          |
|        |              |          |
|        |              |          |
|        |              |          |
|        |              |          |
|        |              |          |

| PACKED | ITEM TO KEEP | LOCATION |
|---|---|---|
|  |  |  |
|  |  |  |
|  |  |  |
|  |  |  |
|  |  |  |
|  |  |  |
|  |  |  |
|  |  |  |
|  |  |  |
|  |  |  |
|  |  |  |
|  |  |  |
|  |  |  |
|  |  |  |
|  |  |  |

| PACKED | ITEM TO KEEP | LOCATION |
|--------|--------------|----------|
|  |  |  |
|  |  |  |
|  |  |  |
|  |  |  |
|  |  |  |
|  |  |  |
|  |  |  |
|  |  |  |
|  |  |  |
|  |  |  |
|  |  |  |
|  |  |  |
|  |  |  |
|  |  |  |
|  |  |  |

Download all forms in printable format for free here:
http://www.formgal.com/thoreauplanners.htm

# 10. Giving Away and Donating Stuff

*"A man is rich in proportion to the number of things he can afford to let alone."* - Henry David Thoreau

 **Donating Forms**

| Completed | This chapter contains the following form; |
|---|---|
| ✓ | |
| | What to Give Away or Donate Form |

The 'What to Give Away or Donate List' is for items you are giving to friends and/or relatives and donating to charities.

**Green:** What to Donate or Give Away List

Depending on the items and the charitable organizations in your area, many of these items might qualify to be picked up at your home at a designated date,

You will want to request receipts if you will be using any of these items for tax deductions.

There are many charity organizations and non-profits that are happy to receive item donations, and many will pick up your donations. These include The Salvation Army, Goodwill, Volunteers of America, your local humane society, and countless more. Many will pick up large bulky items.

## Where to Donate General Household Items

Check your local charities first. Then if needed use the following list of where you can donate specific items.

### *General Donations*

#### Goodwill

About: Breaks down barriers to opportunity by helping individuals build the skills they need to be gain employment.

What to Donate: They need vehicles, clothing, shoes, houseware, books, electronics, etc.

#### Volunteers of America

About: Focuses on providing health and human services to the most vulnerable in our society from the veterans to the disabled, to women and families struggling with addiction.

What to Donate: They need toys, clothes, shoes, appliances, household goods, etc.

#### Salvation Army

About: Operates over 700 social programs including services to the aged and homeless and aims to end poverty by helping build communities internationally.

What to Donate: They need appliances, furniture, clothing, household goods, books, etc.

**Operation Give**

About: Works to empower active and retired members of the Armed Forces to contribute to the lives of those around them through projects such as Builders Without Borders and Operation Christmas Stocking.

What to Donate: They need toys, hygiene items, school supplies, clothes, shoes, etc.

**Vietnam Veterans of America**

About: Helps veterans of the Vietnam war by providing claims assistance, job placement, and using outreach programs to help those suffering from PTSD or drug abuse problems.

What to Donate: They need cloths, furniture, electronics, bikes, toys, books, exercise equipment, tools, etc.

**The Help Kenya Project**

About: Breaks the cycle of poverty by providing education and training to Kenyan students.

What to Donate: They need electronics, clothes, tools, sports equipment, books, etc.

**Cause USA**

About: Provides massages, hospital game carts, special events and entertainment libraries to ill and wounded military members and their families.

What to Donate: They need gift cards, craft supplies, and anything on their Amazon Wishlist.

## Forgotten Soldiers Outreach

About: Sends "We Care" packages to overseas members of the Armed Forces.

What to Donate: They need hygiene items, treats, snacks, and letters of encouragement.

# Where to Donate Clothing and Accessories

## Clothes4Souls

About: Donates clothing to all of those in need around the globe.

What to Donate: They need new and gently-used clothing for children and adults.

## Dress for Success

About: Gives low-income women the clothes and confidence they need to pursue the careers they want.

What to Donate: They need gently used professional women's attire.

## Career Gear

About: Gives unemployed and underemployed men business attire and professional training to pursue the careers they want.

What to Donate: They need gently used professional men's attire.

## The Women's Alliance

About: Provides women with the business attire and professional training they need to attain jobs that allow them to support themselves.

What to Donate: They need gently used professional women's attire.

## Sew Much Comfort

About: Creates and donates adaptive clothing to wounded military men and women to enhance their comfort and dignity.

What to Donate: Clothing of all types for men and women of all shapes and sizes.

## Soles4Souls

About: Provides footwear to those in need.

What to Donate: They need new and gently used footwear.

## Diamonds for Dreams

About: Helps the wishes of patients with metastatic breast cancer come true.

**What to Donate:** They need diamonds, estate jewelry, and other specialty jewelry items.

## Planet Aid

About: Provides health and human services and sells clothing at low-costs to people in developing nations.

What to Donate: They need new and gently-used clothing, shoes, and textiles.

## Where to Donate Wedding and Prom Dresses

### Brides Across America

About: Donates wedding dresses to low-income brides of the Armed Forces.

What to Donate: They need new or gently used wedding dresses from the past three years.

### DonateMyDress.org

About: Gives dresses to low-income girls for special events such as prom, father daughter dance, or quinceanera.

What to Donate: They need special-event dresses for girl.

### Brides Against Breast Cancer

About: Raises breast cancer awareness and grant wishes to patients and their loved ones.

What to Donate: They need new and gently used wedding dresses from the past decade.

### The Glass Slipper Project

About: Provides Chicago-area students in need with the formalwear they need for prom.

What to Donate: They need new and gently-used prom dresses, shoes, and accessories from the past five years.

## *Where to Donate Baby and Children Items*

### SAFE (Stuffed Animals for Emergencies)

About: Provides stuffed animals for children who have experienced abuse, homelessness, and natural disasters.

What to Donate: They need new and gently-used stuffed animals.

### Newborns in Need

About: Provides low-income and ill newborns with care and comfort items.

What to Donate: They need clothing, toys, textiles, yarn, and thread.

### Touching Little Lives

About: Donates care and comfort items to infants in Ohio.

What to Donate: They need clothing, toys, textiles, yard, thread, and blankets.

### Ronald McDonald House

About: Provides stability and resources to families with hospitalized children, including houses and rooms to regroup and rest.

What to Donate: They need food, toiletries, kitchen goods, entertainment products, toys, etc.

### Toys for Tots

About: Distributes toys to needy children for Christmas.

What to Donate: They need toys.

## Loving Hugs

About: Provides stuffed animals to children in refugee camps, orphanages, war zones, and natural disaster areas.

What to Donate: They need new and gently-used stuffed animals.

## Project Smile

About: Gives emergency responders items to provide children with a sense of comfort in stressful situation.

What to Donate: They need new and gently-used stuffed animals and books; new coloring books and new crayons.

## *Where to Donate Electronics*

### World Computer Exchange

About: Gives computers and other devices to public institutions in developing nations.

What to Donate: They need computers, tablets, software, printers, scanners, etc.

### National Cristina Foundation

About: Provides computer to low-income individuals.

What to Donate: They need computers, tablets, software, printers, scanners, etc.

### Get-Well Gamers Foundation

About: Brings entertainment and comfort to children's hospitals by providing them with video game systems.

What to Donate: They need video games, video game systems, controllers, etc.

## Komputers for Kids

About: Bridges the digital divide between upper- and lower-class children.

What to Donate: They need any electronics that are not household appliances.

## HopeLine from Verizon

About: Donates recycled and refurbished wireless phones to domestic violence shelters and social service agencies.

What to Donate: They need used wireless phones and accessories.

## National Coalition Against Domestic Violence

About: Leads the fight against domestic violence.

What to Donate: They need used cell phones. Laptops, and mp3 players.

## Games for Heroes

About: Sends handheld games to deployed members of the Armed Forces.

What to Donate: They need any handheld video game devices.

## Cell Phones for Soldiers

About: Recycles cell phones and purchases calling cards to members of the Armed Forces.

What to Donate: They need cell phones.

### iOS Device Recycling Program

About: Brings Apple products into classrooms for educational purposes.

What to Donate: They need Apple products.

### Fireside International

About: Brings Apple products to Haiti for educational purposes.

What to Donate: They need Apple products.

### Computer Recycling Center

About: Provides electronics to public institutions and safely recycles unusable items.

What to Donate: They need computer, tablet, laptops, printers, etc.

## Where to Donate Office and School Supplies

### Muscular Dystrophy Association

About: Funds research and programs to support muscular dystrophy patients and their families.

What to Donate: They need computers, laptops, prints, and office supplies.

### iLoveSchools

About: Donates classroom resources to school teacher.

What to Donate: They need anything classroom supplies and equipment.

### Develop Africa

About: Donates books and classroom resources; provides scholarships and job training throughout Africa.

What to Donate: They need new and used school and office supplies.

### Pens for Kids

About: Donates pens to kids in Africa.

What to Donate: They need pens.

Swap4Schools

About: Provides classroom resources to schools.

What to Donate: They need books and other media.

## Where to Donate Books

### International Book Project

About: Provides books to those in need, both domestically and internationally.

What to Donate: They need new and gently used books.

### Global Literacy Project

About: Provides learning opportunities to children and adults, both domestically and internationally.

What to Donate: They need reading books and textbooks.

### Books for Africa

About: Donates books to libraries and classrooms throughout Africa.

What to Donate: They need new and gently used books.

## The Bridge of Books Foundation

About: Donates books to public institutions, foster agencies, and homeless shelters.

What to Donate: They need new and gently used book for children and teenagers.

## Books Through Bars

About: Provides books and educational materials to prisoners.

What to Donate: They need new and gently used books. Please inquire before shipping to ensure your donations fit their needs.

## Darien Book Aid

About: Provides books to disadvantaged learners.

What to Donate: They need new and gently used books. Please inquire to ensure your donations fit their needs.

## Books for Soldiers

About: Donate books to deployed members of the Armed Forces.

What to Donate: They need new and gently used books and other media. Please inquire before shipping to ensure your donations fit their needs.

## BookEnds.org

About: Donate books to low-income and underprivileged

communities through public institutions and charity organizations.

What to Donate: They need new and gently used books for children and teenagers.

### Better World Books

About: Collects and sells books online in order to donate books and fund literacy programs around the globe.

What to Donate: They need new and used books.

### Kids Need to Read

About: Creates a culture of literacy by providing books to underfunded schools.

What to Donate: They need new and gently used books.

## Where to Donate DVDS and CDS

### Kidflicks.org

About: Donate media to children's hospitals throughout the US.

What to Donate: They need DVDs and Blu-rays.

### Musicians on Call

About: Brings live and recorded music to hospital patients.

What to Donate: They need new and gently used CDs, CD players and MP3 players.

### DVDs4Vets

About: Donates DVDs and Blu-rays to veteran's centers, veteran's hospitals, and veteran's nursing homes.

What to Donate: They need DVDs, Blu-rays, and DVD players.

### DiscsForDogs.org

About: Collects and sells DVDs and CDs and donates the funds to the ASPCA.

## *Where to Donate Sports Equipment*

### One World Running

About: Donates running shoes to those in need, both domestically and internationally.

What to Donate: They need new and gently used running shoes.

### Sports Gift

About: Donates sporting equipment and runs sports programs to children in need.

What to Donate: They need sporting equipment.

### Bikes for the World

About: Provides bikes to those in developing countries to increase mobility.

What to Donate: They need new and used bicycles for children and adults.

### Bicycles for Humanity

About: Provides bikes to those in developing countries to increase mobility.

What to Donate: They need new and used bicycles and bike parts, and bicycle safety equipment.

### Opportunity Through Baseball

About: Donates baseball equipment to children in need, both domestically and internationally.

What to Donate: They need all types of baseball equipment.

## *Where to Donate Musical Instruments*

### Mr. Holland's Opus Foundation

About: Donates music instruments to communities in need.

What to Donate: They need new and gently used instruments.

### Operation Happy Note

About: Collects and sends instruments to deployed members of the Armed Forces.

What to Donate: They need new and gently used instruments suitable for travel.

### Education Through Music

About: Provides musical instruments to schools in need.

What to Donate: They need new and gently used instruments.

**Hungry for Music** (https://hungryformusic.org)

About: Expands musical opportunities for children domestically and internationally.

What to Donate: They need instruments in any condition.

**Marching Mountains**

About: Provides schools in Appalachia with musical instruments.

What to Donate: They need new and gently used instruments.

## *Where to Donate Eye Glasses*

**Unite for Sight**

About: Provides eye care for adults and children in developing nations.

What to Donate: They need reading glasses, sunglasses, and more.

**New Eyes for the Needy**

About: Donates eyeglasses to charities who will distribute them in developing nations.

What to Donate: They need new and gently used eyeglasses and hearing aids.

**One Sight**

About: Provides eye care for adults and children in need.

What to Donate: They need new and gently use eyeglasses.

## Where to Donate Cars

### Big Brothers Big Sisters' Cars for Kids' Sake

About: Provides emotional support to at-risk children by helping them build strong bonds with good role models.

What to Donate: They need all types of vehicles.

### National Kidney Foundation Kidney Cars

About: Creates community services, funds public health initiatives, and conducts research related to kidney disease.

What to Donate: They need cars, trucks, boats, and RVs.

### National Foundation for Cancer Research

About: Funds research to find a cure for cancer.

What to Donate: They need cars, trucks, boats, and RVs.

### Purple Heart

About: Enhances the quality of life for all veterans and their families.

What to Donate: They need cars, trucks, boats, and RVs.

### Habitat for Humanity Cars for Homes

About: Builds and refurbishes houses for those in need.

What to Donate: They need all types of vehicles.

### American Diabetes Association

About: Conducts research to find a cure for diabetes.

What to Donate: They need cars, trucks, boats, and RVs.

## Where to Donate Supplies for Arts and Crafts

### The CUREchief Foundation

About: Makes and distributes fabric cloths for cancer patients who want head cover.

What to Donate: They need textiles.

### Care Wear

About: Knits, crochets, and sews baby items for infants in the NICU.

What to Donate: They need textiles suitable for children.

### The Mending Hearts Project

About: Helps mothers with infants in the NICU.

What to Donate: They need textiles, sewing equipment, and handmade fabric items.

### Afghans Etc. for Charity

About: Provides comfort items to children with serious illness.

What to Donate: They need crocheting and knitting equipment and handmade afghans.

### Binky Patrol

About: Gives handmade blankets to children in need.

What to Donate: They need textiles and handmade blankets.

## The Knitting Connection

About: Provides volunteers with materials to make handmade clothes and blankets for infants and children.

What to Donate: They need crocheting and knitting equipment and handmade items.

## A Little Something

About: Provides refugee women with the skills to become self-sufficient.

What to Donate: They need crafting supplies.

## Beads of Courage

About: Helps children with serious illnesses tell their stories through beads.

What to Donate: They need beads.

## The Mother Bear Project

About: Donates handmade bears to children with HIV/AIDS in developing nations.

What to Donate: They need crocheting and knitting equipment, stamps, and packing tape.

## Knots of Love

About: Provides handmade caps to cancer patients and the seriously ill.

What to Donate: They need crocheting and knitting equipment.

**Made 4 Aid**

About: Collects, makes, and sells handmade items to donate funds to Doctors Without Borders.

What to Donate: They need homemade items and arts and craft supplies.

**Many Arms Reach You**

About: Donates handmade blankets to mothers and children in need.

What to Donate: They need crocheting and knitting equipment.

**Children's Healing Art Project**

About: Provides materials and space for children in Portland's children's hospitals to freely express themselves.

What to Donate: They need arts and crafts supplies.

## *Other Charites for Miscellaneous Donations*

**TESSA**

About: Provides mental health services to women and children who have suffered from domestic violence and sexual assault.

What to Donate: They need gift cards and used cell phones.

**National Furniture Bank**

About: Provides furniture to those in need.

What to Donate: They need furniture of all kinds.

**St. Jude's Ranch**

About: Provides a safe environment and hope to children and families in need.

What to Donate: This charity needs recycled non-trademarked greeting cards.

## Overseas Coupon Program

About: Forwards "manufacturer's coupons" to overseas military members.

What to Donate: What to Donate: They need manufacturer's coupons, valid and expired up to two months.

## Indigo Rescue

About: Provide specialized assistance to animals with unique characteristics that make them unlikely to be adopted.

What to Donate: They need jewelry for fundraising events.

## Animal Guardian Network

About: Helps elderly, special needs and hospice animals.

What to Donate: They need used purses, jewelry, and artwork.

## What to Give Away or Donate List

| DONE | ITEM TO GIVE AWAY | RECIPIENT |
|------|-------------------|-----------|
|      |                   |           |
|      |                   |           |
|      |                   |           |
|      |                   |           |
|      |                   |           |
|      |                   |           |
|      |                   |           |
|      |                   |           |
|      |                   |           |
|      |                   |           |
|      |                   |           |
|      |                   |           |
|      |                   |           |
|      |                   |           |
|      |                   |           |
|      |                   |           |
|      |                   |           |
|      |                   |           |

| DONE | ITEM TO GIVE AWAY | RECIPIENT |
|------|-------------------|-----------|
|      |                   |           |
|      |                   |           |
|      |                   |           |
|      |                   |           |
|      |                   |           |
|      |                   |           |
|      |                   |           |
|      |                   |           |
|      |                   |           |
|      |                   |           |
|      |                   |           |
|      |                   |           |
|      |                   |           |
|      |                   |           |
|      |                   |           |
|      |                   |           |
|      |                   |           |
|      |                   |           |
|      |                   |           |
|      |                   |           |

| DONE | ITEM TO GIVE AWAY | RECIPIENT |
|------|-------------------|-----------|
|      |                   |           |
|      |                   |           |
|      |                   |           |
|      |                   |           |
|      |                   |           |
|      |                   |           |
|      |                   |           |
|      |                   |           |
|      |                   |           |
|      |                   |           |
|      |                   |           |
|      |                   |           |
|      |                   |           |
|      |                   |           |
|      |                   |           |
|      |                   |           |
|      |                   |           |
|      |                   |           |

| DONE | ITEM TO GIVE AWAY | RECIPIENT |
|------|-------------------|-----------|
|      |                   |           |
|      |                   |           |
|      |                   |           |
|      |                   |           |
|      |                   |           |
|      |                   |           |
|      |                   |           |
|      |                   |           |
|      |                   |           |
|      |                   |           |
|      |                   |           |
|      |                   |           |
|      |                   |           |
|      |                   |           |
|      |                   |           |
|      |                   |           |
|      |                   |           |
|      |                   |           |
|      |                   |           |
|      |                   |           |

| DONE | ITEM TO GIVE AWAY | RECIPIENT |
| --- | --- | --- |
|  |  |  |
|  |  |  |
|  |  |  |
|  |  |  |
|  |  |  |
|  |  |  |
|  |  |  |
|  |  |  |
|  |  |  |
|  |  |  |
|  |  |  |
|  |  |  |
|  |  |  |
|  |  |  |
|  |  |  |
|  |  |  |
|  |  |  |

Download all forms in printable format for free here:
http://www.formgal.com/thoreauplanners.htm

# 11. Selling Your Stuff

*"Most of the luxuries, and many of the so-called comforts of life, are not only dispensable, but positive hindrances to the elevation of mankind."* -- Henry David Thoreau

 **Selling Your Stuff Forms**

| Completed ✓ | This chapter contains the following form; |
|---|---|
|  | What to Sell List |

If you have decided to sell some of your stuff, you can sell these items using any of the following:

- Garage or Yard Sale
- Online Auction such as eBay
- Craigslist and Classifieds
- Facebook Marketplace
- Consignment Shop
- Flea Market
- Estate Sale
- Auction

## Garage or Yard Sale

If you have never held a garage or yard sale, you need to know the work that is required to be successful. A garage or yard sale is similar to operating a retail sales business or store for a day or a few days. After you read the following descriptions and recommendations then you can decide if this is for you.

## Planning Your Sale

Plan where you will display your goods. When you set up your sale in the garage your stuff is protected from the weather and you can hold the sale for several days or more than one weekend if needed without moving items.

A yard sale depends on the weather although if you do not have a garage or more things to sell than will fit in a garage this might be your next choice. Just keep in mind you will need to set everything up early in the morning and at the end of day the put everything away that does not sell.

If there are a lot of smaller items, you might need folding tables to display them.

Note: While turning items into cash can be satisfying, exciting, if you are a care giver or relative conducting or helping with the sale, the owner might find watching potential buyers dig through their belongings upsetting. In this case you can provide support or suggest that your parent, or the person, stay inside the home during the sale or not be there at all.

## Set the Dates

Choose dates and times for your sale. Make sure you have enough advance time to set up your sale, advertise, and get any required permits. Check with your local municipality as some allow sales only during certain months, on specified days during particular times. Some governments have garage and yard sale information and applications online.

Most people shop sales on weekends with Saturday morning being the most popular time. In some areas you can add Thursdays or Sundays your sale.

Start as soon as 7 A.M. on Saturday and be ready for those early birds. Do not be surprised if people begin showing up at 6 A.M. You can either accommodate them or put up a sign that states you do not open until 7 A.M. sharp. Unless there is a reason to stay open longer, I usually close my sales by 2 P.M.

Depending on the seasons where you live, a spring and summer sale are usually best, and fall is next.

## How to Advertise Your Sale

You can put up a sign in your yard and on local streets where legally permitted, directing people to your sale. Be sure to remove them when your sale concludes.

Use brightly colored or neon poster board. Make your print large and legible from a distance. Use the word 'SALE' draw an arrow pointing ion the direction and the address. You

can post on telephone poles or use the free paint stir sticks for placing signs in the ground.

Post your sale on any local news websites and Craigslist. Give the address and times. You can also list larger items, collectibles, and a general description of any other items. Other websites to consider for advertising as of this writing:

- Yard Sale Search
- Garage Sale Hunter
- Yard Hopper
- Garage Sale Source

Let any organizations you belong to such as your church, clubs, bowling league, etc. know about your sale.

If you have a popular local newspaper you can also purchase a classified ad. Because some news sites and papers charge per word, keep your ad short and clear with the dates and address. Run these types of ads just two to three days in advance of your sale and the day of your event.

If you have a Facebook account or other social media accounts, you can also post the news about your sale there.

## How to Price Your Items

While you might think some items have no value, a quick search on eBay and Craigslist can be surprising. People buy cell phone chargers, USB cables, printer cables, blank CDs, and other items you might think no one has a use for. You can also search 'retail arbitrage' on YouTube to discover what people are selling and for how much.

On the other hand, you do not want to overprice your items. Base your prices on what similar items are selling for not your sunk costs (what you paid) or your emotional attachment. Those have no relation to the value of most items. Some people want to haggle so have a discount in mind, say 10% off, that you are willing to accept.

In order to make change easily, I price everything rounded to the nearest dollar or quarter. That way I do not need dimes, nickels and pennies.

Mark everything with the price and keep a log of the prices next to each item on your list. This way if a price sticker or tape comes off and goes missing, you can refer to your list if needed. Using masking tape for price tags is a less expensive tip.

Price your items individually versus by the box or bag.

When you price all your items add up the total. This can help you decide if a garage or yard sale is worth your time. For example, if I do not have at least one thousand dollars' worth of items I do not have a sale. I look for alternative ways to sell my stuff.

## Safety

If your sale is in the garage move any low hanging items where someone could bump their head. Also make sure walkways and aisles are clear.

Be sure your homeowner's insurance is up to date and that you have coverage for visitors for personal injury.

Do not keep a cash box in sight. Keep a small amount of change available.

Always have two people watching your sales at all times. A second person can help you answer questions, negotiate prices or accept payments, and prevent issues such as theft.

Keep your cell phone with you at all times for any emergencies.

## Accepting Credit Cards

I have never accepted credit cards at my garage sales, however, some people do. Shoppers can fund mobile wallets from their bank accounts or use credit cards. E-wallets include PayPal and Venmo, and mobile payment systems such as Google Pay, Apple Pay, Square, Apple Pay, and more. As a garage or yard sale seller you need to know the terms and transaction fees for each one.

For instance, Square currently charges a 2.75 percent fee for each transaction using swiped cards and a 3.5 percent plus 15 cent fees for manually keyed-in payments.

149

Venmo, is owned by PayPal, and free if you and the other party both have Venmo accounts. Otherwise the fee is 3 percent.

Apple Pay allows iPhone or Apple Watch users to pay for their transactions through the devices and you will pay a 3 percent fee per transaction.

## Supplies

Prepare cash for change. You will need at least:

- 20 each one-dollar bills
- 10 each five-dollar bills
- 10 each ten-dollar bills
- 10 each 20-dollar bills
- 20 dollars' worth or quarters

Again, when you round all prices to the nearest dollar or quarter you should not need dimes, nickels and pennies.

## Setting Up

Keep breakables out of reach or children if possible. Set up tables or flat surfaces to display items: these can be card tables, folding tables, saw horses and flat plywood or particle board, etc. I have seen the tops of freezers, washers and dryers, pool tables, furniture, pick-up truck beds, and car hoods covered with sheets or tablecloths serving as display tables.

You can place miscellaneous items in boxes and laundry baskets.

You can hang clothes on garment racks, wires, rope and garage door hangers.

Categorize items when possible. Group clothes, books, home goods, dishes, tools, toys, DVDs and CDs, and collectibles together. Group clothes by children, men and women.

Have everything prepared the night before. If you are having a yard sale have everything organized together inside and ready to set up outside. Map out where everything will be so that you can quickly set up your sale.

## The Big Day

Again, be ready for those early birds. People often arrive an hour before opening looking to be first to get the good deals.

Allow an hour before you open to set everything out, place signs, and set up your chairs. You can also place balloons and signs in your yard making your place easy to spot.

Set your chairs where you can see people coming and can greet them. Try to be where you can see all your items also. Keep your phone handy, drinks, and change. I keep my twenties, tens, and fives in separate pockets. This makes finding the right change easy and I am not flashing a large amount of money around. When I my sales reach a few hundred dollars I place the money in a secure location inside my house.

When you have a garage or yard sale you will be dealing with the public. Some people will engage in conversation, some will not, others might complain about something and occasionally you might get a bad element. Be prepared to retreat into your home, record license plates, and call authorities if needed. In all my years of hosting sales, I have never had such an issue.

I like to stay seated, greet people, let them browse, answer questions, *and collect money.*

## Should You Haggle?

I am less likely to come down in price on my belongings in the first few hours of a sale.

If you do not like to haggle, you can do what I often do and tell hagglers and/or put up a sign that gives 25% off (or whatever you choose) everything the last day or hour of your sale. This not only avoids the haggle but can work very well to help you get rid remaining items at the end of your sale.

After your sale you can count up your cash. Donate leftovers or sell them through one of the following other methods. Be sure to thank any and all helpers, remove any signs, and delete any ads if needed.

## Online Auction such as eBay

You can sell most any item on eBay. I use eBay for my more expensive items such as antiques and collectibles. I

like items that have enough value to make this worth my time and that are easy to pack and ship.

Your collectible and vintage items will commonly get the best prices. Other items that might seem obsolete or unusable to you, could have a market. You can determine what is selling and the value of items by checking out similar items in the eBay marketplace.

## Craigslist and Classifieds

If you have not used Craigslist to buy or sell this is the most popular online classifieds. Setting up an account and placing ads is free.

Choose the correct category for your ad and upload any appropriate images. Your ad will generally go 'live' within 10 minutes or so.

## Consignment Shop

Consignment shops put your item up for sale in their store for a price that gives them a profit over and above an amount you agree to accept for the item.

A specialty shop that focuses on similar items is best. For example, if you have purses to sell, a women's boutique or clothing shop would be a good fit.

If you are in a hurry or moving out of the area this might not be the best choice. However, if your price is right, some consignments will buy your item(s) so be sure to ask if they will.

## Flea Market

If you have a popular local flea market, you can rent a booth and haul your items to the market on the sale day. Due to the cost of rental, needing to pack and haul items, then stay at the market, this is not my first choice.

If you do choose this option, be sure you have items that have enough value to compensate you for your cost. If you have a lot of such items and a cargo trailer or truck this can be a viable choice.

## Facebook Marketplace

The Facebook Marketplace is a convenient way to sell in your area. You can list items and reach thousands of people in your community. You will see people are selling clothes, electronics, cars and real estate.

The Facebook Marketplace is available in the Facebook app and on desktops and tablets. Look at the bottom of the app on iOS or at the top of the app on Android. If using a web browser, you can find the Marketplace on the left side of the Facebook page. You can use Marketplace on iPhone 5 or later, Android and iPad with the Facebook app or on your desktop at www.facebook.com/marketplace.

People can only see the information that you publicly share on Facebook. You get to decide how much information to share. Use Facebook Messenger or communicate via Marketplace to avoid spam and phishing. Facebook advises not to share your personal or bank information.

## Estate Sale

An estate sale is another option. Contrary to common belief, an estate sale is not only for people that have passed. An estate sale is not much different than a yard or garage sale except most everything stays in place inside your home and the weather has little affect. You clean your home, stage certain items if you wish, and block rooms or areas where you do not want traffic.

You can hire an estate sale company or conduct your own sale.

### Hiring an Estates Sale Company

An estate sales stills takes some work. If you want to hire a professional to handle your estate sale check statesales.net and look for a firm that has a good reputation and reviews.

As a rule of thumb, estate sales professionals require a minimum dollar value of goods to take on a sale. This can be $10,000 or more.

Review any contract carefully. Make sure you understand the commission amount, (30 per cent is common), and how you will be paid and when. Typically, estate sales do not bring top dollar for your items.

You need to mark anything you do not want sold and hand a list of these items to the estate sale company.

You need to be present if possible when the estate sales professional and team show up to price and set up your sale.

You want to be available to answer any questions and verify values and histories of some items.

Leave your home during the sale. Shoppers might be noisy, complain, and even rude. You are paying someone to handle all this for you.

## Conducting Your Own Estate Sale

There are a few keys to holding a successful estate sale, and they are as follows:

Create an inventory list of everything in your home including what you will not be selling. Keep notes about the condition of each item. Clean your belongings and repair any broken items that you can.

Check websites that sell similar items, thrift stores, Craigslist, and eBay to establish the values. For expensive items such as highly collectibles or jewelry you might want to seek out an appraiser. When prices are difficult to determine err on the high side. You can always come down for a haggler.

Mark each item with the price. You can use stick labels or even masking tape. You can put similar items together and place a sign in front or over them, for example, all DVDs fifty cents each.

## Off-Limit Items and Areas

Place 'Not for Sale' signs on any items that will not be for sale. Lock or block any off-limit areas in your home.

## Create Safe Traffic Flow

Set up your home in way that allows people enough room to browse without impeding traffic wherever possible.

Placing items along walls or on tables can help. Try not to stack items and place them in a way that makes the prices visible.

## Security

Do not run an estate sale alone. Ideally you should have a person at every entrance and exit and in view of every room. Watch for any theft.

Keep all money in a secure lock box and always supervised. Keep expensive items in one location always under a watchful eye. Every helper should have a cell phone handy at all times.

As with a garage or yard sale, make sure the homeowner's liability policy is up to date and paid for.

## Advertise Your Estate Sale Like Crazy

Your ads should begin about a week in advance of your sale. Local papers, Facebook groups, online classifieds such as Craigslist are all great places to advertise.

Headline your ads with 'Estate Sale' even if the only category is garage sales. Use pictures wherever you can of the items that will appeal to people. Furniture, appliances, antiques, unusual items, and collectibles all attract shoppers. Take well lighted pictures. Most cell phones now produce high quality photos.

You can put up a sign in your yard and on local streets where legally permitted, directing people to your sale. Be sure to remove them when your sale concludes.

Use brightly colored or neon poster board. Make your print large and legible from a distance. Use the words 'ESTATE SALE' draw an arrow pointing ion the direction and the address. You can post on telephone poles or use the free paint stir sticks for placing signs in the ground.

## After the Sale

Remove all signs. Call charities to pick up remaining items you will give away and pack the rest to store or move.

## What to Sell List

Enter the items you will sell on the following 'What to Sell' list and mark each one with a white sticker. Write the price on the list and sticker if you have an idea of what you will ask for the item. If not, you can just mark the item with a white sticker or piece of masking tape and enter the price later.

## What to Sell List

| SOLD | ITEM TO SELL | PRICE |
|------|-------------|-------|
|  |  |  |
|  |  |  |
|  |  |  |
|  |  |  |
|  |  |  |
|  |  |  |
|  |  |  |
|  |  |  |
|  |  |  |
|  |  |  |
|  |  |  |
|  |  |  |
|  |  |  |
|  |  |  |
|  |  |  |
|  |  |  |
|  |  |  |
|  |  |  |

| SOLD | ITEM TO SELL | PRICE |
|------|-------------|-------|
|      |             |       |
|      |             |       |
|      |             |       |
|      |             |       |
|      |             |       |
|      |             |       |
|      |             |       |
|      |             |       |
|      |             |       |
|      |             |       |
|      |             |       |
|      |             |       |
|      |             |       |
|      |             |       |
|      |             |       |
|      |             |       |
|      |             |       |
|      |             |       |
|      |             |       |

# Thoreau's Downsizing Planner for Seniors

| SOLD | ITEM TO SELL | PRICE |
|------|--------------|-------|
|      |              |       |
|      |              |       |
|      |              |       |
|      |              |       |
|      |              |       |
|      |              |       |
|      |              |       |
|      |              |       |
|      |              |       |
|      |              |       |
|      |              |       |
|      |              |       |
|      |              |       |
|      |              |       |
|      |              |       |
|      |              |       |
|      |              |       |
|      |              |       |
|      |              |       |

| SOLD | ITEM TO SELL | PRICE |
|------|--------------|-------|
|      |              |       |
|      |              |       |
|      |              |       |
|      |              |       |
|      |              |       |
|      |              |       |
|      |              |       |
|      |              |       |
|      |              |       |
|      |              |       |
|      |              |       |
|      |              |       |
|      |              |       |
|      |              |       |
|      |              |       |
|      |              |       |
|      |              |       |
|      |              |       |

| SOLD | ITEM TO SELL | PRICE |
|------|--------------|-------|
|      |              |       |
|      |              |       |
|      |              |       |
|      |              |       |
|      |              |       |
|      |              |       |
|      |              |       |
|      |              |       |
|      |              |       |
|      |              |       |
|      |              |       |
|      |              |       |
|      |              |       |
|      |              |       |
|      |              |       |
|      |              |       |
|      |              |       |
|      |              |       |

| SOLD | ITEM TO SELL | PRICE |
|------|--------------|-------|
|      |              |       |
|      |              |       |
|      |              |       |
|      |              |       |
|      |              |       |
|      |              |       |
|      |              |       |
|      |              |       |
|      |              |       |
|      |              |       |
|      |              |       |
|      |              |       |
|      |              |       |
|      |              |       |
|      |              |       |
|      |              |       |
|      |              |       |
|      |              |       |
|      |              |       |

| SOLD | ITEM TO SELL | PRICE |
|------|--------------|-------|
|      |              |       |
|      |              |       |
|      |              |       |
|      |              |       |
|      |              |       |
|      |              |       |
|      |              |       |
|      |              |       |
|      |              |       |
|      |              |       |
|      |              |       |
|      |              |       |
|      |              |       |
|      |              |       |
|      |              |       |
|      |              |       |
|      |              |       |

Download all forms in printable format for free here:
http://www.formgal.com/thoreauplanners.htm

# 12. Storing Your Stuff

 **Storing Your Stuff Forms**

| Completed ✓ | This chapter contains the following form; |
| --- | --- |
| | What to Store List |

One objective of downsizing is to reduce the amount possessions you own. Needing storage for items can conflict with the concept of downsizing. Avoid renting storage space for possessions unless necessary. Paying for storage space is a financial loss most of the time.

However, you might need to store some things temporarily during your move. If you do store items make a deadline date of when you will move, sell, give away, or discard these items. Steer clear of signing any long-term storage agreements.

If you are going to store items, choose a location near where you are going to move.

Storage Considerations

- Accessibility
- Cost
- Location and Accessibility
- Value of items
- Insurance

Deciding where to store your belongings, choosing a facility and a storage unit size, and finding the best way to pack and store your things are important for making sure your items are accessible and not damaged.

## Planning

Decide what items you need stored and how you will pack them. I prefer plastic containers or totes that are stackable. Seal plastic boxes keep your things clean, prevent mold problems and keep any insects and rodents out. Numerous insects make their homes in cardboard and some lay eggs in the corrugation. The last thing you want to bring into your new place one day.

Decide what items and boxes will go where in the storage unit. If you will need any items while in storage place these at the front where they will be accessible. Place heavier containers on the bottom and lighter items on top.

Use paper or bubble wrap to pack fragile things. Label all containers on the sides where you can still read the label when they are stacked.

## *Clothing*

You can use wardrobe boxes to hang clothing when needed. Clothes should be sealed in plastic to prevent moisture or insect damage. I place moth balls in my storage unit and replace them as needed when storing clothes.

## Appliances

Darin water from washing machines and dishwashers and defrost refrigerators before storing. Make sure they are dry inside and out. You can clean them with bleach spray if they will be stored in a high humidity environment where mold is likely.

## Other Items

Wrap or tape stiff cardboard around any pictures and mirrors safe. Wrap these in plastic or bubble wrap to prevent damage and keep insects out. Mark these items as 'Fragile.'

If anything is disassembled place all nuts, bolts and other small components in plastic bags and tape the bags to the corresponding item where you will find them easily.

Cover upholstered and wood furniture with sheets or plastic.

You can put your bedding and draperies in vacuum bags for more space and preservation.

Lightly coat tools with oil to prevent any rust during storage. You can wrap them in garbage bags, pack, and mark all sharp objects as 'Sharp' to prevent injury.

Use the following 'What to Store List' to record everything that you pack and store. Take pictures before pacing for reference and in the case of an insurance claim.

Avoid placing any highly flammable liquids in storage. If you are in an area where the temperature goes below freezing, avoid storing liquids that can freeze.

Clean your barbeque grill and racks thoroughly burning off grease and food. If you use propane remove the tank.

All lawn equipment such as tractors, lawn mowers, trimmers, and clippers should be cleaned and stored per manufacturer recommendations. All fuel must be drained gas from tanks.

Clean outdoor furniture and allow it to dry thoroughly before storing.

While this might take up a bit more space, I like to inflate soccer, footballs, and basketballs, etc. to prevent cracking.

Bicycles should be clean and also thoroughly dry. If the bicycle will be stored for a long time, you can lightly oat any chrome and oil the chain to prevent rust and let some air out of the tires from tires.

## What to Store List

| DATE STORED | ITEM TO STORE | LOCATION |
|---|---|---|
| | | |
| | | |
| | | |
| | | |
| | | |
| | | |
| | | |
| | | |
| | | |
| | | |
| | | |
| | | |
| | | |
| | | |
| | | |
| | | |
| | | |
| | | |

| DATE STORED | ITEM TO STORE | LOCATION |
|---|---|---|
| | | |
| | | |
| | | |
| | | |
| | | |
| | | |
| | | |
| | | |
| | | |
| | | |
| | | |
| | | |
| | | |
| | | |
| | | |
| | | |
| | | |
| | | |

| DATE STORED | ITEM TO STORE | LOCATION |
|---|---|---|
| | | |
| | | |
| | | |
| | | |
| | | |
| | | |
| | | |
| | | |
| | | |
| | | |
| | | |
| | | |
| | | |
| | | |
| | | |
| | | |
| | | |
| | | |

| DATE STORED | ITEM TO STORE | LOCATION |
|---|---|---|
|  |  |  |
|  |  |  |
|  |  |  |
|  |  |  |
|  |  |  |
|  |  |  |
|  |  |  |
|  |  |  |
|  |  |  |
|  |  |  |
|  |  |  |
|  |  |  |
|  |  |  |
|  |  |  |
|  |  |  |
|  |  |  |
|  |  |  |
|  |  |  |

# 13. Discarding Your Stuff

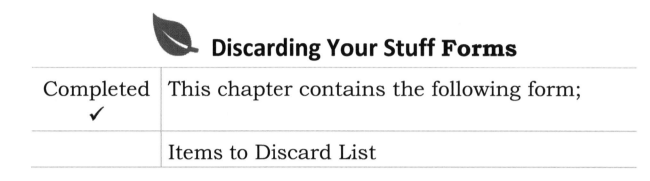
### Discarding Your Stuff Forms

| Completed ✓ | This chapter contains the following form; |
|---|---|
| | Items to Discard List |

Throwing things out seems simple enough however you might want to sort and label items you will discard. In many areas you are required to recycle certain items and hazardous materials require special attention. Organize your waste into the following 5 categories:

- Trash
- Recycle
- Hazardous Materials
- Electronics
- Large Bulky Items

## Hazardous Waste

The EPA considers some leftover household products that can catch fire, react, or explode under certain circumstances, or that are corrosive or toxic as household hazardous waste. Products, such as paints, cleaners, oils,

batteries, and pesticides can contain hazardous ingredients and require special care when you dispose of them.

To avoid the potential risks associated with household hazardous wastes (HHW), it is important that people always monitor the use, storage, and disposal of products with potentially hazardous substances in their homes. Improper disposal of HHW can include pouring them down the drain, on the ground, into storm sewers, or in some cases putting them out with the regular trash.

The dangers of such disposal methods might not be immediately obvious, but improper disposal of these wastes can pollute the environment and pose a threat to human health. Certain types of HHW have the potential to cause physical injury to sanitation workers, contaminate septic tanks or wastewater treatment systems if poured down drains or toilets. They can also present hazards to children and pets if left around the house.

Check with your local environmental, health or solid waste agency for more information on HHW management options in your area. If your community doesn't have a year-round collection system for HHW, see if there are any designated days in your area for collecting HHW at a central location to ensure safe management and disposal.

If your community has neither a permanent collection site nor a special collection day, you might be able to drop off certain products at local businesses for recycling or proper disposal. Some local garages, for example, may accept used motor oil for recycling. Check around.

Even empty containers of HHW can pose hazards because of the residual chemicals that might remain so handle them with care also.

## Recycling Electronics

Many trash and disposal companies as well as landfills do not accept electronic items. Donating and recycling is a great way for you to help conserve resources and natural materials.

It is important to make sure you are donating and/or recycling electronics safely and correctly.

Before you donate or recycle your used electronics delete all personal information from your electronics and remove any batteries. Batteries require separate recycling. For more information and to find out where you can donate or recycle electronic goods visit:

https://www.epa.gov/recycle/electronics-donation-and-recycling

## What to Discard List

| DONE | ITEM TO DISCARD | CATEGORY |
|------|-----------------|----------|
|      |                 |          |
|      |                 |          |
|      |                 |          |
|      |                 |          |
|      |                 |          |
|      |                 |          |
|      |                 |          |
|      |                 |          |
|      |                 |          |
|      |                 |          |
|      |                 |          |
|      |                 |          |
|      |                 |          |
|      |                 |          |
|      |                 |          |
|      |                 |          |
|      |                 |          |
|      |                 |          |

| DONE | ITEM TO DISCARD | CATEGORY |
|------|-----------------|----------|
|      |                 |          |
|      |                 |          |
|      |                 |          |
|      |                 |          |
|      |                 |          |
|      |                 |          |
|      |                 |          |
|      |                 |          |
|      |                 |          |
|      |                 |          |
|      |                 |          |
|      |                 |          |
|      |                 |          |
|      |                 |          |
|      |                 |          |
|      |                 |          |
|      |                 |          |
|      |                 |          |
|      |                 |          |

| | ITEM TO DISCARD | CATEGORY |
|---|---|---|
| | | |
| | | |
| | | |
| | | |
| | | |
| | | |
| | | |
| | | |
| | | |
| | | |
| | | |
| | | |
| | | |
| | | |
| | | |
| | | |
| | | |
| | | |
| | | |

| | ITEM TO DISCARD | CATEGORY |
|---|---|---|
| | | |
| | | |
| | | |
| | | |
| | | |
| | | |
| | | |
| | | |
| | | |
| | | |
| | | |
| | | |
| | | |
| | | |
| | | |
| | | |
| | | |
| | | |

## Why Should You Replace Some Items?

When you are downsizing your stuff, there are some items that might need to be replaced or that you should replace.

The most obvious items to replace are those that are broken and irreparable or badly outdated. But you might also replace some items that need to be downsized. For example, you might no longer need a dining table with 8 chairs and replace that with a smaller table and fewer chairs.

Or you might want to save space by getting something new that replaces several items. For instance, there are many new kitchen gadgets that perform multi-functions and there are brooms that are also mops. Some new items are now smaller and updated with more features than their predecessors.

## What to Replace List

| DONE | ITEM TO REPLACE | REASON |
|------|-----------------|--------|
|      |                 |        |
|      |                 |        |
|      |                 |        |
|      |                 |        |
|      |                 |        |
|      |                 |        |
|      |                 |        |
|      |                 |        |
|      |                 |        |
|      |                 |        |
|      |                 |        |
|      |                 |        |
|      |                 |        |
|      |                 |        |
|      |                 |        |

Download all forms in printable format for free here:
http://www.formgal.com/thoreauplanners.htm

# 14. How Can You Get Your Documents and Records in Perfect Order?

*"We must learn to reawaken and keep ourselves awake, not by mechanical aids, but by an infinite expectation of the dawn, which does not forsake us even in our soundest sleep. To affect the quality of the day, that is the highest of arts."* – Henry David Thoreau

 **Documents and Records Forms**

| Completed ✓ | This chapter contains the following form; |
|---|---|
| | Important Documents List |

Getting all your important documents and records in order is a good idea any time but is crucial before you move. During a move documents and records are often misplaced and lost or even accidently thrown away.

When you are a relative is dealing with any crisis the last thing anyone wants to be doing is searching through a storage locker, basement or dusty attic, anxiously looking for a vital document, or spending time in attorney or government offices filling out forms to try and obtain replacement papers.

Legally-binding paperwork, records, and forms can be needed in a variety of situations including:

- Moving to a senior community
- Seeking a loan
- Being hospitalized
- Being displaced by an emergency or natural disaster
- Applying for state, federal or veteran benefits
- Selling property or your home
- Facing litigation
- Insurance claims

Your adult children will greatly appreciate being able to locate all your essential documents you might need in an emergency. Knowing where all your documents and official records are located and keeping copies available can save you literally thousands of dollars in some cases and time spent looking for documents.

## The Issue of Privacy

Many seniors guard their financial information with a degree of privacy and often do not discuss money with their adult children. Unfortunately, in times of crisis this secrecy can cause unnecessary expenses, stress, and time for relatives. If a senior develops dementia, memory loss, other illness or passes away suddenly, the relatives can be left sorting out financial matters for years to come.

Tell your loved ones and or trusted advisors where your crucial information is located. Collect and keep together your important papers such as deeds, wills, Durable Powers of Attorney, medical records, and those records on the following 'Important Documents List'. Keep them in a safe, file cabinet or safe-deposit box. Inform your key family members or attorney where you keep these documents. If you are downsizing into a care or support facility a safe deposit box at a local bank is recommended.

Shred all unneeded papers that contain personal or identifying information. If you are not sure about any financial records, ask your accountant or tax preparer what records to keep.

## Healthcare Documents You Need

When a person is debilitated or can no longer communicate, a living will (also known as a healthcare directive), can dictate his or her wishes and designate someone for representation. Health care workers and Doctors need paperwork that shows durable power-of-attorney or an advanced-health-care-directive.

In addition, having your medical history readily available could save your life in an emergency, and at the least are often required when seeking benefits and Medicaid, or relocating to a care facility.

**Important health care documents:**

\_\_\_\_ Health care proxy (durable health power-of-attorney)

\_\_\_\_ Authorization to release health-care information

_____ Living will (healthcare directive)

_____ End-of-Life and Estate Planning Documents You Need

_____ Personal medical history

_____ Insurance card (Medicare, Medicaid, Independent)

_____ Long-term care insurance policy

## Important End-of-Life Documents:

_____ Will

_____ Trust documents

_____ Life-insurance policies

_____ End of life instructions letter (regarding wishes not covered in will for example, regarding memorial, or other items not covered in the will)

_____ Organ donor card

## Other Necessary Documents

There are numerous other documents and records that are necessary for a myriad of situations. Use the following Important Documents List to organize your paperwork.

## Important Documents List

| Location | Documents |
|---|---|
| | Deeds |
| | Mortgages |
| | Will |
| | Power of Attorney |
| | Birth Certificates |
| | Passports |
| | Diplomas |
| | Degrees |
| | Military Records |
| | Certificates |
| | Medical Records |
| | Contacts List |
| | Loans |
| | Insurance |
| | Investments |
| | Stocks and Bonds |
| | |
| | |
| | |
| | |

| Location | Documents |
|---|---|
| | Auto Title |
| | Auto Title |
| | Boat Title |
| | RV Title |
| | User Names and Passwords |
| | Business Interests |
| | Pets |
| | Livestock |
| | Government Benefits |
| | Child Support Orders |
| | Debt Documents |
| | Passports |
| | Marriage Certificates |
| | Divorce Certificates |
| | Court Orders |
| | Employment Contracts |
| | Legal Settlements |
| | Passports |
| | Promissory Notes Held |
| | Loan Documents |
| | Vehicle Registrations |

| Location | Documents |
|---|---|
|  | Mutual Funds |
|  | Bank Records |

| Location | Documents |
|---|---|
|  |  |
|  |  |
|  |  |
|  |  |
|  |  |
|  |  |
|  |  |

| Location | Tax Records |
|---|---|
|  | Federal and State Income Tax Records |
|  | Business Tax Records |
|  | Property Tax Records |
|  |  |
|  |  |
|  |  |
|  |  |

Download all forms in printable format for free here:
http://www.formgal.com/thoreauplanners.htm

# Section V. Moving

# 15. Address Change

*"What lies behind us and what lies ahead of us are tiny matters compared to what lives within us."*
- Henry David Thoreau

## Address Change Forms

| Completed ✓ | This chapter contains the following forms; |
|---|---|
|  | Address Change Checklist |

### Do you need a PO Box?

You might want to get a PO Box if you will be:

- hitting the road in an RV
- moving into a Tiny House
- staying somewhere temporarily
- need additional privacy

### Change Your Address with the Postal Service

- Go to USPS.com/move to change your address online. This is the preferred method for speed and convenience, and you immediately get an email

confirmation of the change.
https://moversguide.usps.com/icoa/home/icoa-main-flow.do?execution=e1s1&_flowId=icoa-main-flow&referral=MG82

- Go to your local post office and request a Movers Guide.
https://tools.usps.com/go/POLocatorAction_input

You can also ask the USPS to temporarily change your address

https://www.usps.com/manage/forward.htm

Or to hold your mail:

http://holdmail.usps.com/holdmail/

**Change Your Address with Other Government Agencies**

Other federal and state agencies to contact when changing your address include:

**Internal Revenue Service (IRS)**
Contact the IRS to change your address if you are expecting a tax refund or other mail. You can also change your address with the IRS by writing your new address in the appropriate boxes on your tax return when you file.

http://www.irs.gov/Help-&-Resources/Tools-&-FAQs/FAQs-for-Individuals/Frequently-Asked-Tax-Questions-&-Answers/IRS-Procedures/Address-Changes/Address-Changes

**Social Security Administration (SSA)**
Change your address online using my Social

Security account if you receive Social Security retirement, survivors, or disability benefits or are enrolled in Medicare.
**Link:** http://www.socialsecurity.gov/myaccount/

## Department of Veterans Affairs (VA)

Contact the VA if you are a veteran who receives benefit payments, or you wish to update your records.
Link:
http://iris.custhelp.com/app/answers/detail/a_id/3045/

## U.S. Citizenship and Immigration Services (USCIS)

Contact USCIS if you are a non-U.S. citizen who is required to register your address.

**Link:** http://www.uscis.gov/addresschange

## State Motor Vehicle Agencies

Contact your state to change your address on your driver's license or motor vehicle registration.

**Link:** https://www.usa.gov/states-and-territories

## State Election Offices

Contact your state election office to change your address on your voter registration record.

**Link:**
http://www.eac.gov/voter_resources/contact_your_state.aspx

## Address Change Checklist

| Date to Do | Done | Address Change Notification |
|---|---|---|
| | | Old Post Office |
| | | New Post Office |
| | | Post Office Box Rental |
| | | Driver's License: |
| | | Driver's License: |
| | | Voter Registration: |
| | | Voter Registration: |
| | | Medicare: |
| | | Medicare: |
| | | Social Security: |
| | | Social Security: |
| | | Bank: |
| | | Bank: |
| | | Retirement Account: |
| | | Retirement Account: |
| | | Retirement Account: |
| | | Financial Adviser |
| | | |
| | | |

| Date to Do | Done | Address Change Notification |
|---|---|---|
|  |  | Credit Card: |
|  |  | Credit Card: |
|  |  | Credit Card: |
|  |  | Credit Card: |
|  |  | Credit Card: |
|  |  | Loan Account: |
|  |  | Loan Account: |
|  |  | Insurance Agent: |
|  |  | Insurance Agent: |
|  |  | Auto Registration: |
|  |  | Auto Registration: |
|  |  | Auto Registration: |
|  |  | RV Registration: |
|  |  | Boat Registration: |
|  |  | Club or Association: |
|  |  | Club or Association: |
|  |  | Charity |
|  |  | Charity |
|  |  | Charity |
|  |  |  |
|  |  |  |

| Date to Do | Done | Address Change Notification |
|---|---|---|
| | | Place of Worship |
| | | Employment: |
| | | Employment: |
| | | Alimony or Child Support |
| | | Legal Settlement: |
| | | Other Legal: |
| | | Newspaper/Subscriptions |
| | | Property Tenants |
| | | Money Owed to You: |
| | | Money Owed to You: |
| | | Lawyer |
| | | Accountant |
| | | Caregiver: |
| | | Physician: |
| | | Physician: |
| | | Health Insurance: |
| | | Health Insurance: |
| | | |
| | | |
| | | |
| | | |

| Date to Do | Done | Address Change Notification |
|---|---|---|
| | | Optometrist |
| | | Dentist |
| | | Orthodontist |
| | | Volunteer Association: |
| | | Volunteer Association: |
| | | Volunteer Association: |
| | | Cell Phone Service |
| | | Cell Phone Service |
| | | Alma Mater |
| | | Alma Mater |
| | | School |
| | | Daycare |
| | | Veterinarian |
| | | Department of Veterans Affairs |
| | | U.S. Citizenship and Immigration Services USCIS |
| | | |
| | | |
| | | |
| | | |
| | | |

| Date to Do | Done | Associates, Friends, and Family |
|---|---|---|
| | | |
| | | |
| | | |
| | | |
| | | |
| | | |
| | | |
| | | |
| | | |
| | | |
| | | |
| | | |
| | | |
| | | |
| | | |
| | | |
| | | |

Download all forms in printable format for free here:
http://www.formgal.com/thoreauplanners.htm

# 16. Things to Stop or Shut Off

## Things to Stop or Shut Off Forms

| Completed ✓ | This chapter contains the following form; |
|---|---|
| | Utilities to Stop, Transfer, or Shut Off Checklist |
| | Home Services to Stop or Transfer Checklist |

Make a list of each utility company and home service and their addresses and phone numbers. Set a date for two weeks before you will move to cancel or transfer your utilities and home services. Use the 'Utilities to Stop, Transfer, or Shut Off Checklist' and the 'Home Services to Stop or Transfer Checklist' to track your progress.

## Utilities to Stop, Transfer, or Shut Off Checklist

| Date to Do | Completed | UTILITIES TO STOP, TRANSFER, OR SHUT OFF |
|---|---|---|
| | | Electric |
| | | Gas |
| | | Propane |
| | | Water |
| | | Heating Oil |
| | | Sewer |
| | | Cable |
| | | Internet |
| | | Telephone |
| | | Refuse or Trash Pick Up |
| | | Recycling |
| | | **Other Utilities** |
| | | |
| | | |
| | | |
| | | |

## Home Services to Stop or Transfer Checklist

| Date to Do | Completed | HOME SERVICES TO STOP OR TRANSFER |
|---|---|---|
|  |  | Security / Alarm System |
|  |  | Lawn Sprinkler Agreement |
|  |  | Lawn Care Agreement |
|  |  | Pest Control Agreement |
|  |  | Snow Removal Agreement |
|  |  | Chimney Sweep Agreement |
|  |  | Homeowner's Association |
|  |  | Well Inspection Agreement |
|  |  | Newspaper Delivery |
|  |  | Heating/AC Maintenance Agreements |
|  |  | Housekeeping or Maid Service |
|  |  |  |
|  |  | **Other Home Services** |
|  |  | Food Services Delivery |
|  |  | Support Services |
|  |  |  |
|  |  |  |
|  |  |  |

# 17. Packing

 **Packing Forms**

| Completed ✓ | This chapter contains the following form; |
|---|---|
| | Packing Checklist |

## Where to Get Boxes

Moving companies frequently have specialized containers such as wardrobe boxes.

### Free Boxes

### Office Supply Stores

Office supply stores such as Office Max often have packing material and boxes.

### McDonald's Fry Boxes

McDonald's fry boxes are strong and excellent for packing heavy items that fit in a smaller sized box. The fries are shipped frozen so there is no smell or grease.

### Starbucks

Starbuck's stores generally receive one or two shipments each week and the boxes range in size.

## Bookstores

Books are shipped in boxes of all shapes and sizes and are strong. Check local colleges as they often have book stores too.

## Bars and Restaurants

Restaurants receive vegetables, liquor, canned goods, etc. in boxes they discard.

## Grocery and Liquor Stores

Check with your local grocery and liquor stores for when their shipments come in and if you can pick up some boxes from them.

## Pharmacies

Walgreens, CVS, or Rite Aid are most everywhere and will have boxes when they receive shipments.

## Home Improvement Stores

Stores such as Lowes and Home Depot will frequently have many large boxes.

## Other Options

**Craigslist/Freecycle** – Community-based online forum.

**U-Haul Box Exchange** – U-Haul's free message board for people to find used boxes for free.

**Recycling Centers** – Some recycling centers have lightly used boxes for reuse.

## Where to Buy Boxes

- Your moving company

- U-Haul
- UPS Store or Other Pack and Ship Store
- Online – Retailers and discount hubs have bundles of boxes for discounted prices.
- Lowes, Home Depot, etc.

## Packing and Labeling

Label all boxes by their destination room or area where the contents will go in your new residence. Add a label to necessities such as bathroom items as 'Open First.' Include items such as bedding, soap, toilet paper, toothpaste & toothbrush, towel, plate and utensils, a change of clothes, flashlight, tape, pen or pencil and scissors.

Label boxes as 'Important Items' that contain your new lease or residence contract, keys, medications, legal documents, checkbook, cell phone, address book, first-aid kit, and your Thoreau's Downsizing Planner'.

## Packing Checklist

| DONE | PACKING ACTION ITEM |
|------|---------------------|
|      | Complete stuff lists and label all belongings |
|      | Obtain boxes |
|      | Obtain packing materials |
|      | Obtain markers and /or labels |
|      | Obtain scissors and packing tape |
|      | Label and pack 'Open First' boxes |
|      | Label and pack 'Important Items' |
|      | Ensure that all boxes are properly labeled. |
|      |  |
|      |  |
|      |  |
|      |  |
|      |  |
|      |  |
|      |  |
|      |  |

# 18. Moving

*"Never look back unless you are planning to go that way."*
- Henry David Thoreau

 **Moving Forms**

| Completed ✓ | This chapter contains the following form; |
| --- | --- |
|  | Preparing to Move Checklist |

Coordinate your move for a non-peak moving time if possible. These dates vary based on seasons and location. Generally, the best time of the month is in the middle of the month. Most people move on weekends that fall at the end of or first few days of the month.

Once you have set a firm date for the move, get estimates from moving companies. When you are getting estimates from moving companies, the fees are often negotiable. This is especially the case when you can plan and schedule your move for a nonpeak time.

Create a floor plan of your new residence with 'to scale' measurements with doors, windows, appliances, shelves, closets, air vents, etc. Measure your larger items such as furniture and know where these will be placed.

## Preparing to Move Checklist

| DONE | PREPARING TO MOVE ACTION ITEM |
|------|-------------------------------|
|      | Rent a new safety deposit box near your destination residence if needed. |
|      | Refill any prescriptions in advance. |
|      | Get estimates from moving companies and select one. Get a firm time for the mover's arrival, at both the old and new residences. |
|      | Be sure you have a written contract from the moving company with clear language of coverage for lost or damaged possessions and how long you have after the move to make a claim. (Allow for time to unpack.) |
|      | Make all pet arrangements for moving them and their accommodations in your new home. |
|      | Check your floor plan of your new home and decide where all large items will be placed. |
|      | Ensure you have all keys for your new residence. |
|      | Plan to have someone to meet the movers at your new residence with a key. If your new residence is a community be sure to alert the manager. |
|      | Make sure all utilities will be available at your new residence on your moving date. |

# 19. Welcome Home

*"The setting sun is reflected from the windows of the alms-house as brightly as from the rich man's abode."*
- Henry David Thoreau

 **Welcome Home Forms**

| Completed ✓ | This chapter contains the following form; |
|---|---|
| | Keys Organization Form |
| | Safety Checklist |

Locate your 'open first' boxes for your bedroom, bathroom, and kitchen immediately. Then take your time and spend a few days unpacking and organizing.

As you are unpacking if you discover any items are missing or damaged during the move, contact your mover in writing and in accordance with your agreement with them and include pictured if the damaged items if applicable.

If you cannot reach a settlement with your mover, you may have the right to request arbitration from your mover. Arbitration is not mandatory for you, but it may be for your mover.

You may choose to pursue a civil action in an appropriate court having legal jurisdiction in lieu of arbitration.

## Check Keys

Keys might not be one of the first items that come to mind when moving though you need to have your locks changed as soon as you move in to your new home. If you are renting the property, check with your landlord or property manager first.

Keys are one of the items you will use most, and lost or misplaced keys can cost you money and time, so this is an opportunity to make sure your keys are organized, accessibly located and that you have 'back ups' or copies.

If you have had to search for lost or misplaced keys, you know the time that can be spent and stress this can cause. In addition, if you have ever been locked out of your car or home and had to break in or call a locksmith you are familiar with how much losing your keys can cost you.

Losing keys, getting locked out, and emergencies that require the right keys are most all preventable. There are many key organization methods to help you.

Here are my 7 steps for organizing your keys:

## The 7 Steps for Organizing Your Keys

1) Label All Keys

2) Keep Keys Handy and Secure

3) Make Duplicates of Keys and Know Where They Are

4) Store Important Keys Off Site

5) Give Access Keys to Someone You Trust

6) Use Appropriate Key Chains and Holders

7) Use technology to Track Your Keys

## Keys Organization Form

| Key To / Quantity | Assigned to or Location of Key | Duplicate Given to or Location |
|---|---|---|
|  |  |  |
|  |  |  |
|  |  |  |
|  |  |  |
|  |  |  |
|  |  |  |
|  |  |  |
|  |  |  |
|  |  |  |
|  |  |  |
|  |  |  |
|  |  |  |
|  |  |  |
|  |  |  |
|  |  |  |
|  |  |  |
|  |  |  |

## Safety First

Any home requires specific safety items be in place, operational and accessible. Reviewing safety items before spending one night in your new home could save your life.

- Smoke alarm and carbon monoxide alarm operation
- Security system
- Fire extinguisher
- Phones and emergency numbers
- First aid kits
- Flashlights
- Home inventory
- Vehicle license plate numbers and VINs (Vehicle Identification Numbers)
- Night Lights
- Fire Ladders
- Personal Protective Equipment

Locate your new home's circuit breakers, gas shut-offs, and all water shut-offs including a main water shut off if applicable. You will always want a flashlight on your night stand from your first night in your new home. Your surroundings will be unfamiliar in the dark and there will be plenty of obstacles such as boxes during your first few nights.

**Note:** If you smell natural gas or propane do not attempt to search for a shut off but exit the home immediately and contact authorities.

## Safety Checklist

| Done ✓ | Item and Action |
|---|---|
| | **Smoke Alarms:** Check that they are operational and accessible for turning off in a non-emergency and to change batteries. Note on a calendar, appointment book, or set a phone alarm to change these twice a year. |
| | **Carbon Monoxide Alarms:** Check that they are operational and accessible for turning off in a non-emergency and to change batteries. List these on a calendar, appointment book, or set a phone alarm to changes these twice a year. |
| | **Security System:** Check to that system is operational and accessible for turning off in a non-emergency and to change any batteries. List these on a calendar, appointment book, or set a phone alarm to changes these twice a year or as recommended by security company. |
| | **Fire Extinguishers:** The kitchen, garage, bedrooms, and basements are all good places to locate fire extinguishers. Get the right extinguishers for the most likely fires in each area. These items do expire so mark on your calendar or set an alarm on your phone for when they need to be replaced. |

## Clean Before Unpacking

While your new residence might be clean, if you are like me you might want to be sure everything is up to your standards. Cleaning before you unpack and place all your belongings is easier now than later. You should have packed a priority 1 box with basic cleaning supplies. Bedroom, bath, and kitchen are usually the first rooms to get populated with belongings so do clean those rooms first.

## Locate Boxes and Unpack by Priority

Bedroom, bathroom, and kitchen are the most important to unpack first.

Instead of tackling everything set up only what you will need for the next day or two. In the kitchen for example you might want napkins, paper towels, a frying pan, a toaster, a coffee maker (a must!), plates, cups and basic silverware. In the bathroom unpack your priority boxes of toiletries and towels.

## Paperwork

See the chapter 'How Can You Get Your Documents and Records in Perfect Order?' You should already have all your paperwork in order if you have the print hard copy version of this book or if you have the print copies of the forms from this book, available for free at:
http://www.formgal.com/thoreauplanners.htm

## Unpacking

When you are rested begin by unpacking one room at a time. Break down and remove packing material and boxes as you go. Recycle anything you can.

While unpacking, you might find items that you were on the fence about keeping when you packed. Now is the perfect time to declutter and get rid of any items you either do not want or that will not be in keeping with the décor or space in your new home.

If you come across stuff that needs to go in storage or another room do so immediately. The goal is to have each room 100% unpacked and organized as you go. Don't leave things to put away 'later' that will only create clutter.

## Make Yourself at Home

Hang your pictures, put your personal items and claim your new space. Adjusting to a new environment is different for each person. As soon as possible establish your routine. Consistency will help you begin to feel at home. This can take days, weeks, or even months. A new place can take time to become 'Home Sweet Home.'

After downsizing you might miss certain items though you like most people you will probably feel a great sense of relief. Many 'downsizers' say "I should have done this many years ago!"

**If you have any questions or comments, please contact us at:**

http://www.formgal.com/thoreauplanners.htm

Thank you for getting Thoreau's Downsizing Planner for Seniors

*I wish you the best with your downsizing!*

If you have comments, or see information in this book that needs updating, please contact:
phil@tweetside.com

# Notes

Thoreau's Downsizing Planner for Seniors

# Resources

**AARP**
601 E St., NW
Washington DC 20049
(888) 687-2277

**Administration for Community Living**
U.S. Department of Health & Human Services
330 C St., SW
Washington, DC 20201
(202) 401-4634

**Aging Life Care Association** (formerly the National Association of
Professional Geriatric
Care Managers)

**Alzheimer's Association**
225 N. Michigan Ave., Fl. 17
Chicago, IL 60601-7633
(800) 272-3900

**American Bar Association**
Commission on Law and Aging
202.662.8690
www.abanet.org/aging/resources/statemap.shtml

**Eden Alternative**
P.O. Box 18369
Rochester, NY 14618
(585) 461-3951

**Eldercare Locator**
Locate Area Agencies on Aging and other resources
(800) 677-1116

**LongTermCare.gov**

**Medicare and Medicaid**
(800) MEDICARE

**National Center for Assisted Living**
Offers Choosing an Assisted Living Residence: A Consumer's Guide

**U.S. Department of Housing and Urban Development**
Housing Counseling Agency
451 7th St., SW
Washington, DC 20410
(202) 708-1112

**Village to Village Network**
(617)-299- 9NET

**Moving On:** A Practical Guide to Downsizing the Family Home, Hetzer, L. and Hulstrand, J., 2004, Stewart, Tabori & Chang Publishers

**National Association of Senior Move Managers**

Professional association of U.S. organizations assisting older adults and families with downsizing, relocating and home modifications. www.nasmm.org

**Senior Move Managers**

Online resource for families seeking assistance with late-life home transitions, such as moving, downsizing and remodeling. www.moveseniors.com

35495162R00122